THE CUSTOMER SUPPORT HANDBOOK

How to Create the Ultimate Customer Experience For Your Brand

Plus stories and advice from the web's leading support experts

Revised edition

SARAH HATTER & CoSUPPORT

The Customer Support Handbook

Cover and identity design by Chad Bercea

Edited by Jason Rehmus With contributions by Richard White, Spencer Fry, Laura Gluhanich, Jason Rehmus, Shervin Talieh, and Jeff Vincent.

First Printing: 2014
Second Printing: 2018

ISBN 978-0615962016 (CoSupport)

CoSupport, LLC

www.cosupport.com

CONTENTS

INTRODUCTION: AN ODE TO THE SUPPORT TEAM

You're reading this book for a few reasons:

- You do customer support for a living and have no resources to improve your work
- Someone you look up to mentioned it on Twitter
- You just liked the cover (it's ok to admit it)

Whatever the reason you found this book and decided to read it, I want to start by telling you one thing: If you're working in customer support, ***what you do matters.*** This book was written to remind you of that, and to let you know that your job is real, it's important, and it's really, really needed.

If you're a CEO Or Founder: This book is your primer on the future of customer support - not just offering transactional service but intentionally striving to make your company's customer service the new gold standard. Learn about the importance of engaging your customer support team with your product development, how to really measure customer happiness, and why you should be investing in your support staff as your top rung employees.

If you're a customer support professional: This book is your validation, your reminder that what you do for a living is an important part of product development and the future of the web. Learn tips and tricks for offering the best customer support possible, including example replies for tough questions, recommendations on better language and tone to use in social media, and advice on handling difficult customers.

CoSupport was started to give people a voice—not just myself because I wanted prove that I had good ideas and could be successful—but everyone like me who works in customer support for the web. I wanted to prove that customer support is incredibly important and valuable, and has to be given a seat at the table. Customer support is marketing. It's R&D. It's the bottom line of your financials. Customer support is, truly, your entire product. There are a lot of people out there who still think such things are nonsense, but I don't.

I quietly observed weird inequities in the web world for a long time before launching CoSupport in 2011. I would notice that product managers would spend months plotting new features or improvements, and right when they were ready for launch they'd bring in the support team for a primer on what changed. I would notice that development teams would have long conversations about adding or removing features without consulting the support team on the potential fallout. I noticed that a junior Rails developer had an average starting salary of $90k while support agents typically brought in $45k a year.

But it was the support agent who was up in the middle of the night, furiously apologizing to customers for a bug the junior Rails developer introduced. It was the support agents who had to explain why a feature changed, not the product manager. It was the support agent who had to defend design decisions, and write help articles explaining how a product works, and tell the development team a feature was difficult to use. It was the support agent keeping tabs on complaints, feature requests, daily support volume, and overall customer happiness. It was the support department dealing with irate customers after a price increase or manually refunding erroneous billing charges.

I remember once having a long, difficult discussion about this with my boss at the time, explaining that I felt my role wasn't ever given consideration during product development. I'd spent the last 6 months at that job slowly cracking apart, trying to get my voice heard by a company that simply wasn't interested in hearing it. We raised our voices and shook our fists at each other, and finally he shouted, *"You want to be equal to developers but you're not! They are the ones who matter!"*

Three days later I filed papers to create CoSupport, LLC. Because, you see, no one in this process matters more—developers aren't better than designers and designers aren't better than support and managers aren't better than janitors. To have a successful product and successful team, you have to consider that everyone is equal in what they bring to the table. When companies realize that their support team is a valuable asset in the lifecycle of their development, everyone wins.

When your support team is an afterthought, or a second-class citizen, so are your customers. Customers deserve better. They deserve your time and attention and empathy. The team that delivers that to customers, day in and day out, deserves your respect.

Our goal at CoSupport is to legitimize the role of a customer service department to not just be a low-paying job for uneducated masses but a really important facet of any company wanting to make a difference.

These days, I spend a lot of my time mentoring support agents and community managers, and training them to find their voice. You can't just talk loudly, I've learned; you need to have something to say to get people to listen. There's no school for customer support, so we started UserConf, now called The Elevate Support Summit, our twice-annual conference just for support teams. Anyone who interacts with customers as their main job now has a chance to learn from experts in the field and a place they can go to see how legitimate and important and relevant their job is.

And now we've written this book, so when you're away from Elevate you have a manual of all our tips, tricks, stories and suggestions. Everything I've ever said in a training session, or on stage at a conference, or in a webinar or podcast about support is right here. You don't have to read it all in order, and we included easy reference pages at the end.This book is here to guide you, encourage you, motivate you, and remind you that you are so very, very *important.*

You may not hear this enough from people you work with, so I want to say it again: **your job is real** and it's **important**. I know it's a hard job, and sometimes you feel very isolated and lonely. I know it stings to see developers or designers get the accolades and attention when you're just as deserving of praise for your job. Customers complain to you all day long and you listen and reply gracefully. You spend a good chunk of your day fixing things, and apologizing for things you didn't cause, and trying to make customers happy.

I know that rarely do people from other departments say, *"Good job,"* but they do say, *"I don't know how you do it everyday."* I know that you just want to have a little bit of an ego boost every now and then and be told you're amazing. I know that you want to feel like your job is at the top of the totem pole, and not a lower role to be thrown at an intern to do for free.

This is for you to remember when you read this book:

YOU ARE WONDERFUL

Even if no one tells you and no one notices.
Your job is so hard, and you do it so well.

You're a small part of making the web better, and making people happy, and that matters more than praise or ego or recognition. Your voice is important, and it needs to be heard.

And in case you haven't heard this lately,

THANK YOU.

ESSAYS

"Our DNA is as a consumer company - for that individual customer who's voting thumbs up or thumbs down. That's who we think about. And we think that our job is to take responsibility for the complete user experience. And if it's not up to par, it's our fault, plain and simple."

— Steve Jobs

"Most of what makes a book 'good' is that we are reading it at the right moment for us."

— Alain de Botton

BLAME IT ALL ON MR. SELFRIDGE

You may not recognize his name, but Harry Gordon Selfridge is probably the reason you have a career in customer support and service. Over 100 years ago, Selfridge began instituting radical ideas about the consumer experience that have become commonplace today. If you've been to London you've seen his name on the huge department store at the end of Oxford Street, or maybe you watched the Masterpiece series based on his life starring Jeremy Piven. (A much better looking Selfridge than the real life version.)

There's another reason you should know about him. He's noted as being the originator of the most famous phrase related to customer service: "The customer is always right."

Oh, goodness. That phrase. Never has a string of words been so polarizing, so misunderstood or so misappropriated in the world of customer support. Go ahead and Google it and you'll find pages of link-bait articles by tech entrepreneurs expounding on the fault in this sentiment, and how their web company will succeed because their customers won't always be right!

The truth is, the customer is not always, 100% of the time going to be right. What if a customer writes an email demanding they receive your product for free? What if they smear your name on Twitter when you refuse to comply? Is that customer right? What if a customer acts unethically, or with prejudice, or berates or abuses your staff?

These are situations where the customer would be flat-out wrong. But these are not the situations Selfridge, or any of his peers, were referring to when they repeated this mantra. In order to really understand this phrase we have to consider its provenance, and the exact circumstances by which it became so well-known. If you're interested in learning the origins of exceptional customer experiences, or how you can emulate the father of customer support in your role, or if you're just a big history nerd, read on.

BACK IN 1909

When Selfridge and his peers began using this phrase, it was a very different time in the world of customer service. In fact, customers were quite wary of retailers and vendors at the turn of the 20th century, due to unscrupulous business owners and wandering tinkers who routinely sold ineffective junk to unsuspecting buyers. Snake oil salesmen roamed the countryside, Coca-Cola had actual cocaine in it, and redheaded orphans were being cast off and abandoned to drunk bootleggers*. (*Maybe not 100% historically accurate.) It was a very different time.

So Selfridge had a plan when he decided to open his own department store, and that was to restore the customer's faith in the vendor. He wanted to prove that customers could trust the people who sold them goods. He chose to invest first in making the experience of shopping at Selfridges a world-class event for anyone who came through the doors.

Selfridge changed the practice of shopping by implementing food courts, so customers could eat lunch or dinner without leaving the confines of the store. He was the first retailer to incorporate glass display cases and artistic store windows, so customers could browse and window shop without pressure to buy anything. He is the genius person to blame for putting a perfume sprayer at the front of every store, but it was done to mask the smell of horse shit wafting in from those gross old-timey streets. (It may be time for us to chill out on that practice a bit, since none of us are trotting our horses up to Nordstrom anymore.)

We take for granted the luxuries of shopping malls and department stores and the conveniences we're afforded. These things are normal to us now, and we don't even look the other way when we stroll past the Sbarro unless they're having a 2-for-1 slice deal. But in 1909, these were absolutely revolutionary business practices. No one before, not even the great Marshall Field who

Selfridge trained under, had devoted so much attention, money, and planning to the customer's experience.

Selfridge didn't just nonchalantly consider the customer experience when he built his store. He didn't loudly declare his customers would have the best experience, snap his gloved fingers, and it suddenly happened. Selfridge knew that, in order to offer the most remarkable customer experience ever, he had to have the most remarkable staff ever, and that meant finding and training the right people for the job. He was willing to seek out people who were trained in customer and concierge service, and he had no qualms about poaching employees by offering them 10% over their existing pay rate.

Think that's crazy? Selfridge actually lost a good chunk of his initial investors when he decided to hire managers and shopgirls for his store a year before it opened to the public. It was an outrageous notion to hire employees a year before you had actual employment for them, but Selfridge believed his employees needed the time to be trained well. He scrapped together enough new investors who believed in his vision and trudged on. He even caused an absolute scandal in the British press when he marched 50 employees down to the construction site to view progress on his shop. It was unheard of—this flamboyant American hiring shopgirls with no shop, then consulting his new employees on the construction of his namesake store!

Selfridge brought his staff to the construction site because he knew they needed to know the layout of the store better than anyone. Shopgirls needed to direct customers to departments without hesitation, and those departments needed to flow in a cohesive pattern. A manager of the ladies undergarments department would know that the smell of leather goods may turn off potential customers more than a contractor or architect would, so why wouldn't you ask her input? By bringing his actual team to the construction site, Selfridge proved that the customer experience was the most important part of building a company that could thrive, and proved anyone who directly engaged with the customer deserved a voice in how that customer would be engaged.

WHAT THIS MEANS FOR US

Selfridge wanted his peers and competitors to understand that to be a customer is to experience a product as a habitual practice. You don't just walk into a store, buy an item and leave, you actually keep that item and use it and remember what exactly made you purchase it. The same goes for customers who are using our products online—whatever made them find your product, signup for a trial, decide to pay you a fee and then use the product is their experience with your customer support.

When he declared that the customer was always right, he didn't mean any customer could walk into a store, make outrageous demands and be on their way. But he did mean that above and beyond, no-questions asked service was the new standard, and that vendors must consider the entire customer experience first and foremost, and make it a priority.

Customer support is not simply the reply they received from your team explaining how a feature works. It's not a quick live chat conversation, or a mention on Twitter. The best companies know that anything related to how the customer habitually engages with your product is an experience with your support philosophy. Your customer support is every part of a customer interacting with your brand, your company name, your product, and your reputation.

For instance, if I am looking for a collaborative online project space for myself and my team, I'll probably Google those words, then click one of the top links and browse around the page. I'll search for main features, I'll immediately want to know the cost, then I'll see if there's a support forum or help section that's easy to use, then I'll click the Sign Up or Trial page. If there's less than 4 boxes required to signup and start using a trial, I'll enter my info and poke around the app a bit. However, if I have to get an email verification before I can start using a product, I am 89% less likely to start using the trial that day.[1] This entire process is not

---

1 *Numbers based on our user experience testing with live apps during 2012-2013.*

UI, and it's not information architecture, and it's not product design. It's customer support.

My interaction with your customer support begins when I type in the words I'm looking for in a search engine and find your product at the top. That's how marketing is a part of your customer support team. Once I check out your product page, and I'm able to find the features I need at the price I want, that is my second support interaction. So now we've integrated product design into customer support as well. When I check out your support community and find you have a robust help section and forum that's updated daily by helpful support staff, now your actual customer support team has rounded out my support experience.

To Mr. Selfridge, the architecture and design of his building impacted the customer experience from their first step inside. (Does your landing page clearly move a customer through main features to purchase in seconds?) If a customer could see products behind a glass case before making their choice as part of the customer experience, it had a greater impact on whether they would purchase the product immediately or take time to think about it. (Think about this when you send those verification emails!) When a customer could linger at their store all day and have every question asked, every need taken care of, and forget that there were other stores they could visit, their customer experience was complete. (How's your help section looking these days?)

WHY THE CUSTOMER NEEDS TO BE RIGHT, TODAY

So you see, we haven't evolved much since 1909. We're still seeing customers interact with our product in very similar ways, but what is different with how our companies are structured? It's simple: Customer support and the customer experience is the last thing we think about. It's the last position we hire for, and we typically don't even know who to hire for the job. (I once helped hire for a support position where a candidate was evaluated by the CEO as, "She seems really nice and we need a female on our staff page.")

If we want to emulate the way Selfridge envisioned the customer experience, we have to start with the idea that the customer deserves our attention, time, thought, planning, development and concern. The customer needs to feel that their needs are being met first, before they even know they have needs.

When we dig in our heels and declare that we aren't going to let customers determine how we build our products, or if we assume we know better than our customers do of their workflow, we aren't putting their experience first. But when we spend time to invest in our support system before we're in a crisis with customers, we're telling customers they matter. We're telling them, in one way or another, that they're right.

Now, if only your web app could have a food court...

GOING ABOVE AND BEYOND

When you ask people for examples of companies who offer great customer service, what names are you bound to hear? American Express? Nordstrom? Zappos?

All of these companies share some pretty simple philosophies about customer service: They're all known for being friendly and personal, for going above and beyond (even for small things) and all have transparent and flexible service-based ideals like free shipping, no questions asked returns, and they hire *professional* customer service employees. These companies are in a completely different class of customer service than, say, the returns line at Walmart, and it's easy for us to immediately *feel* what's different.

Here's the secret: There is absolutely no reason your company—or even Walmart—can't have customer support as stellar and as well-loved as any one of these companies. Your customers could very well talk about your support team just as people rave about Zappos, or be evangelists for your brand just as AmEx customers are. It just takes some time, some effort, and a decision to go above and beyond the basic *transactional experience* with customers.

Let's take Zappos as an example. The little online shoe company has blossomed into so much more than an online retailer, mostly thanks to their stellar reputation of making their customers *happy*. That's it. That's their very unique and brazen philosophy about customer service: *Make customers happy.*

What makes their customers happy? An easy-to-use website. Free overnight shipping. No questions asked on returns, and free return shipping if you send something back. Super helpful customer service agents. And we've all heard the story of the Zappos employee who stayed on the phone with a customer for hours, just chatting away, until the customer was ready to end the call. (There's even a famous story of a Zappos employee ordering pizza for a customer who called their support line, but by now we know it was most likely not a common occurrence since that caller was none other than their founder and CEO.)

People hear these stories and have their own great experiences with Zappos customer service, and next thing you know they're raving like maniacs! I've never heard a bad thing about them from anyone. But I'm going to share a secret with you: I don't think Zappos is that great at customer service. I think that 99% of online customer service is so wretched, so disastrous, and so infuriating that any company can stand out if they just put in a little extra effort. Zappos has put in some effort—not too much, but *just enough* to make them stand out.

Let's further break down these support practices and identify what's really going on:

- Zappos makes the customer's experience the most important thing, even if that means staying on the phone a bit longer than normal and having a friendly chat with a customer.
- Zappos offers free next-day shipping to customers, and pays for return shipping if you need to send something back.
- Zappos has a goal to make sure all customers are happy.

Do these sound like revolutionary business practices? In plain text, they are actually completely reasonable, achievable support standards that any online company could implement *right now*. So why aren't more companies doing exactly what Zappos is doing, and excelling just as they are? It's easy to give Zappos-quality support to your customers even if you don't have their unlimited budget, unlimited staff, and their established reputation.

THE REAL WORLD EXPERIENCE

When I think about my experiences as a customer of a web app, I always relate it back to a real life experience in a brick-and-mortar store. We've all had really bad customer service experiences in stores, but more often than not we don't get *any* customer service at all. Take for instance CVS Pharmacy. Going to CVS is a miserable experience for everyone. No one gets excited to go to CVS or plans a special trip there. You don't get on the CVS website looking for new arrivals and then plan to visit your local store to see it in person. CVS is a place you have to go to out of necessity, usually at the precise moment of your necessity.

I was at a CVS recently and absolutely marveled at what a terrible experience it was. The fluorescent lights flickered overhead, and garbled announcements over the PA interrupted a bad Avril Lavigne song which, incidentally, would make any experience anywhere pretty unbearable. Navigating the aisles left me perplexed—there's no reason cat food and bleach need to share a shelf, right? And then, there I was in a makeshift line with 5 or 6 other souls, between a ten-for-$1 circus peanuts candy bin and a display of old off-brand chocolates. The guy in front of me had it worse, holding tight to a single can of tuna and an enormous jug of Imodium. (Perhaps he was launching a preemptive strike against that generic lemon tuna?)

When it was finally my turn to pay for my bobby pins, shower cleaner, and the shampoo I was in dire need of, the cashier didn't even greet or acknowledge me. She looked off into the distance, the great wild west of the endless CVS store, and with robotic precision checked and bagged my items and tallied the total, all without breaking eye contact with the horizon. I paid her cash, a machine dispensed my change, and that was that.

What a terrible experience

It's no wonder people hate the very idea of contacting a website's customer support when their real life experience with customer support is so blatantly terrible. We can't very well blame the people doing this job, though. It's a bad job to begin with, usually reserved for those with little work experience or interest in dealing with people. And a chain like CVS certainly doesn't care enough about the customer experience to train their employees in excellent service, since they know at the end of the day some poor guy will need to come through their door and buy Imodium from them, regardless of how he's treated during the experience.

Soon after my CVS adventure, I went to J.Crew. I've shopped at J.Crew a lot because overall it's a pleasant experience, even if I don't purchase anything. As I walked in I compared J.Crew to walking into a CVS and was taken by the difference. The store was wide and bright and inviting from the street. Huge windows pulled fresh daylight into the store that spilled elegantly over perfectly presented clothes, all hanging in color order.

Almost as soon as I walked in I was greeted by an employee who stopped folding cardigans and turned her entire body my direction. I let her know I was looking for something specific—a sundress and matching jewelry—and she walked me over to the section herself. As I was trying on some things, she came back to offer me a sweater she thought I might like as well since, as she noticed, it matched my green eyes.

Wow. *What a contrast.* Here was someone not only trained to treat customers with kindness and attention, but also someone who obviously enjoyed her job and was chosen because she did. Not only that, the entire environment of the store screamed out that the customer experience was important and they wanted to make it as pleasant as possible—they didn't mind if you were just browsing. If we take this idea back to how support is done on the web, we see a huge gap between companies who hire people who love helping people and invest in training them, and companies who hire whoever will do the job for low pay.

We have all these contrasting experiences now—CVS vs. J.Crew or Walmart vs. Zappos—and when we put them side by side it's clear what make these experiences different: One set of retailers put something into the experience while the other set doesn't invest in anything more than offering low prices. One set thinks about the entire customer experience while the other thinks about the transactional experience.

So what's stopping more companies from bringing amazing customer support to their products? We have all this time and money invested in these apps, so why is the support experience still so bad? It's so bad because the people building these apps don't think of it as a priority. Instead, support is an afterthought, documentation is done on the fly after an app is launched, and founders opt to just do support themselves instead of paying someone trained in support who can do it well. We see cool new apps launch all the time, and soon after the main page will declare, *"We're hiring a support person!"* Funny, they never think about this *before* launch.

If we started thinking about the online support we offer as CVS vs. J.Crew, of course we'd want our company to be the better brand in the scenario and offer more friendly help and education than our competitor. It may be difficult to think of ways you can stand out, but it gets easier if you keep coming back to the thought, *"Is this a Zappos experience or a CVS experience?"* If you're wondering where you'd even start, here are a few tips to get started offering much better support.

- **Commit to being personable in your communication.** Write to each customer as you'd write to a friend, using lighthearted words like "Hi" and "Awesome idea!" Each time you end an email, invite your customer to write back if they need more help and thank them for being a customer. If you're not always positive or have a cheerful attitude, take the time to write yourself some canned responses you can reuse when you're not feeling inspired. We all have bad days, but don't let that influence how you communicate with you your customers.
- **Treat all your customers like VIPs.** No customer should ever know that you're buried in support

emails or that you really don't care about their feature request. Any customer who interacts with your team should get a friendly, thoughtful reply, no matter what. Remember how you love being treated by a company and what makes you feel like a special customer. Was it someone who was patient with you on the phone while you figured something out? The next time you're on a customer call, emulate that person! Was it someone who replaced your broken iPhone without any questions asked? Try giving out refunds or returns with the same policy. Maybe you loved a coffee shop because they always remember your favorite drink. Each time you answer an email from your customers, see if the person wrote you before, and start the email with, *"Hi again!"* Go above and beyond for the small things: extending a customer's free trial, following up with them a week later to see if they need more help, recognizing them on social media, company blogs or newsletters.

- **Consider the entire experience.** If you think customer support is just the moment you reply to an email, you're doing it wrong. Your customers experience your support system when they search your help section, follow you on Twitter, or read your customer forums. Think of the ambiance you'd want your company to have if it were a real store, and the brand recognition you'd want your products to have if customers experienced them as physical objects.

It's simple: Happy customers reward you with their loyalty. Exceptional customer service converts into customer loyalty. It converts into raving fans who will praise your team on Twitter, and Facebook, and talk about their experience over lunch with friends. There is no greater marketing for your product than happy, surprised, raving fans, and no reason you can't start now.

THANK YOU FOR YOUR FEEDBACK

Breaking bad habits around customer support and service starts with identifying common constructs of our relationships with customers that are failing. One of those is those failing practices is the language we're using in emails, on phone calls and live chat, and even in social media. A phrase all of us has heard a hundred times and repeated back to our own customers without ever thinking it was unacceptable is, *"Thank you for your feedback."*

At our company, CoSupport, we only have two rules we work and live by: We are unwaveringly kind to our teammates and we don't thank people for their feedback. Almost everyone I've hired has heard me say at one point, *"If you ever use this phrase, I will fire you."*

So far, none of our employees has thanked me for my feedback on this matter.

As someone who has been an archetypal customer her whole life, hearing this phrase from a support agent on the other end of the phone makes me cringe. When I see it in print, it's absolutely rage-inducing. This phrase isn't polite and it's not a kind response to someone who's purchased your product. It's robotic, cold, scripted, and is a passive-aggressive way of shutting down a conversation when you simply don't want to deal with it anymore. It tells me you aren't really going to do anything about my problem, but you're going to pretend like you care. It tells me your customers don't have a voice and our opinions don't matter, and you're just going to placate us until we shut up.

When I train executive groups on language for customer support, we spend more time on this one sentence than anything else. At first people are confused that I would demonize it so much, and I usually get my point across by using this analogy: Feedback is the sound a live microphone makes when it gets too close to a speaker. It's the sound that makes everyone in the room cover their ears and duck. And *that's* the word you're using to describe your customer's thoughts about your product.

But even with that analogy, it still can't be *that bad* to thank customers for their feedback, especially since it's actually a *really good practice* to get in the habit of thanking customers for telling us how they feel about anything, good or bad. But that's not what this phrase does—in fact, the only sentence that thanks a customer for telling us how they feel is, "Thanks for telling me how you feel!"

Put the phrases back to back and tell me you don't see a difference:

"Thank you for your feedback."
vs.
"Thanks for telling me how you feel about this!"

Each time we thank customers for their feedback, we're allowing our service language to be dictated by ancient professional standards that were adequate 20-30 years ago. "Thank you for your feedback" is a sentence that people say because they've heard it said before, and it *sounds* like what you're supposed to say, right? If a customer came to your website and saw that in order to buy your product they needed to fax you a copy of their credit card, would that be acceptable? If you're not okay with using ancient, irrelevant technology in your business, why are you okay using ancient, irrelevant language?

In a new age of service design, this phrase is anything but acceptable. So, if we're not going to thank people for their feedback, how are we going to convince customers we're listening? How do we accept our customer's feature ideas or opinions in a more human, more believable way? Off the top of my head, here are some alternatives you can start using today:

Responding to feature requests:

- *"Great idea! Thanks for taking the time to send this one in."*
- *"Thanks for sharing your thoughts on this!"*

Responding to feature requests when you probably aren't going to add the feature:

- *"Thanks for sharing this idea! It's one we've heard before, so we'll make sure it's on our list of features to consider when we're ready to make some changes."*
- *"We don't have plans to offer this option right now, but it's definitely an idea we can come back to when we're adding features to a later version."*

Responding when a customer's had a bad experience:

- *"You're right, we could definitely do this better."*
- *"Thanks for being open and honest about your experience so we can learn from it."*
- *"I really appreciate you helping us improve our process—we don't want this to happen again."*

Those are examples that took me just as long to create as it took for you to read. The difference between those sentences and *"Thank you for your feedback"* is these examples required me to be intentional about the message being sent to the customer. Being *intentional* with language means we're choosing certain words because they mean more to us, and in turn hoping our customers have a unique experience with our service, compared with everyone else who is using outdated, unacceptable language. These phrases don't shut down conversations with customers, the words aren't harsh or uncaring, and the tone is enthusiastic and interested.

Like any new practice, there's going to be a fear to overcome when you start using these very different words with customers. It's going to be uncomfortable using phrases you aren't used to hearing, but that's a part of modifying our approach to customer service. That makes us evolve from using standard, predictable language to using an intentional, human tone in all our communications.

"We see our customers as invited guests to a party, and we are the hosts. It's our job every day to make every important aspect of the customer experience a little bit better."

— *Jeff Bezos*

A FUTURE IN CUSTOMER SERVICE

BY RICHARD WHITE, FOUNDER, *USERVOICE*

For most people, "customer service" doesn't engender warm, fuzzy feelings.

It's not something any of us studied in college.

And it's not likely a career path your parents pushed you towards.

And yet here you are reading a book on customer service. But we're not talking about the "press zero to speak with an agent" call center experience your mom is probably thinking of. We're talking about the exceptional kind of customer service we've come to associate with great brands like Zappos or Amazon. The kind of exceptional customer service that you used to only get from local mom-and-pop stores is now the future of all customer service.

Though I live in San Francisco, this isn't just some hippie nonsense. A number of fundamental shifts in recent years have caused companies to rethink how they invest in and deploy customer service. The result is that many businesses are once again creating cultures of caring. They treat their customers like human beings, respect their intelligence, value their time and ideas, and solve their problems rather than simply funneling them through a process.

So let's walk through these shifts that are the underlying reason why it's worth your time to keep reading this book.

SHIFT #1 - BUSINESSES BUILT ON THE INTERNET ARE BUILT ON CUSTOMER SELF-SERVICE

According to a recent Ask Your Target Market (AYTM) survey commissioned by UserVoice, 43 percent of respondents (62 percent ages 18-24) feel they can solve service issues on their own if companies put better self-service tools in place.[2] But large corporations generally don't do this, which is one reason they often provide such awful customer service. Instead, their customer service agents spend most of their time bridging a digital divide between the consumer and those back-end systems only the agents can reach.

In this more traditional model of customer service, agents aren't empowered to be human or real; they can only turn dials that customers can't turn on their own.

2

That's why they work from scripts. It's human-powered automation, and it's inhumane, both to the agents and to the customers.

Not so for those businesses built from the ground up on the Internet. Their customers have all the dials and switches at their command. If users contact customer service, it's probably because they don't know which dial to turn, not because they can't access it. In this world, there are no scripts because anything that could be scripted has already been automated and made available to the end-user, who now finds it inconceivable that they should have to contact companies to change basic information, like notification settings or credit card information.

According to BT Global Services, 56 percent of online consumers agree that the calls they do make to customer service are much more complex, as simple transactions are often automated. So once you remove those rote tasks, what's left are the exceptional issues that require savvy agents to unpack and solve.

SHIFT #2 - SUBSCRIPTION-BASED BUSINESS MODELS ARE BLURRING THE LINE BETWEEN SALES & SUPPORT

An even more important shift shaping the future of customer service is that more and more companies are adopting subscription-based models, which significantly blurs the line between sales and support.

The move to subscription-based models isn't big news in Silicon Valley, but what's remarkable is how widespread this shift is already, even outside the area. According to Incyte Group, 50 percent of U.S. businesses have adopted or are planning to adopt a subscription-based model. And subscription-based businesses are rendering the traditional sales funnel obsolete.

It used to be that sales people tried like crazy to move consumers from lead to prospect to customer as quickly as possible. That was the hard work. Once prospects became customers, they got locked into multi-year contracts and the business had little reason to spend more time on them. Customers were then handed off to those call centers mentioned earlier.

That's no longer the case. Today, people show up at your digital door, go through a self-service sign-up process, and become paying customers before you even have a chance to enter them in the CRM system. Now it's about trying like crazy to keep these customers. Every (now increasingly complex) customer interaction can easily turn into an upsell opportunity or the potential to lose a customer. Yet another reason savvy companies are staffing their support teams with high quality agents who can handle any issue that comes up—ultimately blurring the lines between sales and support.

SHIFT #3 - SOCIAL MEDIA IS THE CATALYST OF THE FUTURE, IF NOT THE CHANNEL

Of course, it's impossible to discuss the future of customer service without acknowledging the impact social media has had in resetting customer expectations.

By amplifying the voice of the individual, social media has made old school "word of mouth" relevant again. The cost of providing a single bad customer service experience has never been higher, and so the value of providing a great one has never been higher as well.

Companies that want to provide great support now have to adapt to their customers' hours of operation and preferred modes of communication, instead of the other way around.

But for all the hype about social support, there is still little data to back the idea that people prefer to tweet their customer service issues. AYTM's survey indicates that only one percent of respondents prefer to handle their customer support issues over Twitter versus more traditional channels like phone or email.

When companies make more traditional methods of contact easily available on their website, customers rarely turn to Twitter for customer service. Only when companies corrupt traditional channels and aren't responsive (for example, an airline may take two days to return an email but only 20 minutes to answer a

Tweet) do customers flock to Twitter (aka "the small claims court of bad support") to air their grievances.

It's not that customers enjoy asking for help in 140 characters or less. It's that they like the way and the speed in which they are (currently) treated on social channels. And savvy companies are expanding that level of service to all of their channels, not just social media, in order to keep up with this new reality.

SHIFT #4 - THE AGE OF DIGITAL MARKETING GIMMICKS IS COMING TO AN END

A startup I once worked for raised millions based only on the ability to drive millions of people, through somewhat questionable methods, into signing up for its service in a matter of hours. Around the same time, other companies, mostly on Facebook, were "going viral" by tricking users to spam their contact list when they signed up.

But these companies didn't create any real value, and the gimmicks didn't last. The platforms on which they were based eventually closed the loopholes that enabled them to work in the first place.

These weren't isolated incidents. Ever since the Internet took off over 15 years ago, we've spent most of our collective energy coming up with ways to use it to acquire customers more cheaply than ever before.

If you think back to the biggest internet darlings of the last decade, all of them were built on a clever but unsustainable way of acquiring customers. Zynga spammed your Facebook wall. Groupon took advantage of cheap Facebook ads. eHow, and others, milked SEO. But as ever more companies have tilled those soils, they're starting to yield much less than they once did.

Even paid search, easily the crown jewel of internet acquisition channels, doesn't have the huge pockets of untapped opportunities like they used to. ROI on Google Adwords has declined 12 percent annually in recent years, according to eFrontier & Magna Global.

What happens when your cost per click becomes too expensive, your daily deal emails stop being opened, your viral loops get shut down and consumers get burned out on your crappy blogspam content? Trouble. For as good as all of these companies were at acquiring customers they were equally bad at retaining them. Which brings me to my final point.

SHIFT #5 - CUSTOMER RETENTION IS THE NEW ACQUISITION

The path to customer retention is through great products, and great products are born from companies that listen to and understand their users. Great products are also bundled with great customer service, across any medium, at any time of day.

Sixty years ago, consumers could find great customer service at the corner barber shop, the mom-and-pop grocery stores--places where business owners valued keeping the customers they had over acquiring ones they didn't. Places where human connection and conversation, even if they didn't lead to sales, were encouraged.

Where technology once put those companies out of business in favor of larger, less human outfits, today technology is leveling the playing field. Businesses are returning to traditional customer service values, just on a much larger scale. They're treating customers (and potential customers) like humans, not numbers. They're hiring smart customer-facing people, and empowering them to make real decisions and provide real service, instead of working from scripts. And they're engaging customers to learn how they can make their products and services even better.

And the best part is that since no one did go to school for this kind of customer service, you've got a huge head start just by the fact you're even reading this book.

So when your mom asks, you can confidently tell her you don't have a job in customer service, you have a career in it and it's going to kick ass.

HUMANIZING THE WEB

A few years ago, a series of commercials airing non-stop on TV featured a wiry robot on a futuristic assembly line tapping his nubby robot fingers on an Android phone screen. The cameras panned around a shiny metal foreground and an industrial, spaceship-like warehouse, void of all human life. Clearly, someone at the ad agency was taking this "android" theme pretty literally—we get it, it's a robot.

Maybe this is just my sensitivity, or maybe it's because analyzing the way companies present their customer experience is what I do for a living, but even now when I think of Android I think *robotic.* I remember those pokey metal fingers and cold, creaky steel arms. I think *not human.* These commercials didn't convince me to buy an Android, in fact it made me give pretty strong side-eye every time I saw someone use one.

Right now, we're living in the future. We may not have cars that fly but we have some that park themselves. We don't have jetpacks just yet, but Sonos comes pretty close for coolness factor. The future is always supposed to be about innovation and technology, but what we're finding more and more is this future is lacking the human connection. When companies actively start removing human elements from their advertising, it speaks to a whole new mindset that what matters is automation and machinery.

This may be the future, but humans still exist in it. We're still craving the old corner store and the proprietor who knows our name. We're *wowed* by personalization, and we know when something is a cut-and-paste reply. We tell our friends when a big company is friendly and thoughtful. We really just want the person on the other end of the phone to apologize sincerely for the trouble we're having and empathize with our annoyance.

Not too long ago, the comedian Richard Lawson started tweeting his frustrations with Time Warner Cable. The exchange started out pretty tame on his part when he tweeted:

> ***@rlaws:*** *"Thanks, @TWC_Help or whoever for completely failing to do a service I pay you $200 a month to do. Great doing business with you!"*

Time Warner Cable, in all its corporate conglomerate scripted speak replied:

> ***@TWC_Help:*** *"I apologize for the DVR trouble. Can you please DM your account information and we can assist."*

Mr. Lawson, in his growing outrage, replied to Time Warner Cable:

> **@rlaws:** *"DM you my account information? You have my name. Find my account and give me a call. I pay you $2,400 a year."*

Oh my goodness. This isn't going to end well, is it? Keep reading while I go get some popcorn.

He continued his rant further:

> **@rlaws:** *"It's now my mission in life to get whoever works the @TWC_Help account to quit their job and live the life they deserve. You can do it!"*

> **@rlaws:** *"I feel bad for whatever poor jerk is running the @TWC_Help twitter, I really do. But they work for the worst company in the world."*

> **@rlaws:** *"To whatever actual human is running this @ TWC_Help account, I have no ill will toward you. But you work for the devil."*

Ok, by this point there *has* to be someone at Time Warner Cable who wants to really help this guy, *right*?

> **@rlaws:** *"I write about TV for a living. I should be able to rely on the service I pay so much money for to work."*

> **@TWC_Help:** *"Agreed which is why we reached out to you."*

> **@rlaws:** *"No. Tweeting at me after I've complained is not 'reaching out'."*

OH SNAP RICHARD LAWSON!

> ***@rlaws:*** *"Does a robot run @TWC_Help? Is that the problem? If that's the case, I refuse to apologize to robots. My parents taught me better."*

In a final act of total Bozo ignorance, Time Warner Cable replied:

@TWC_Help: *"We are not robots. We are here to assist."*

Sigh. So, what went wrong here? Let's break it down without any more comedic interludes:

- A customer expressed his irritation with a company over social media
- The company responded robotically, without empathy, and asked the customer to do more work to investigate the issue
- The customer doesn't want to do work for the company! They are voicing their frustration and want someone to listen!
- The company continues to respond in scripted, flat language, enraging the customer more
- The customer ends by ridiculing the company and still doesn't get a resolution to his frustration

Many people may read the first reply from Time Warner and think, "What's the big deal? They're trying to help!" Well, people like myself and Richard Lawson aren't having it. We are a breed of new, entitled consumers who expect companies to treat us like royalty. Are we out of line for expecting that? Or are we just really sick of feeling like we're talking to robots?

When I read these tweets from Mr. Lawson, I have to admit inside I jumped for joy. This, *this* is the stuff I *live for*, when huge legacy companies are called on the carpet for not taking the initiative to make a customer's experience better. Look, I understand some companies are bound by legal clauses and may not be able to look up customer info voluntarily, and I understand some are further bound by style guides written by marketing teams who have no experience in customer service. But Mr. Lawson is absolutely right in his annoyance, and while a social media temper tantrum isn't the best way to handle issues like this, he's speaking for a whole mass of consumers who feel brushed off and ignored by corporations who just don't seem to care.

So how *should have* @TWCHelp responded? First, they should have taken it upon themselves to find Mr. Lawson's account information and contact him directly. Does that sound totally over the top to you? Well, it is. That is the point. Second, they should have replied with much more thoughtful language, especially considering their reply was going out into the public ether where it will forever live as a historical record of how Time Warner Cable treats its customers.

If I were tweeting for @TWCHelp, I would have replied to Mr. Lawson's first complaint with something like,

"Oh no! So sorry about that issue. We're reaching out to you now to try and help."

Let's put that back-to-back with @TWCHelp's real reply, shall we?

"I apologize for the DVR trouble. Can you please DM your account information and we can assist."

vs.

"Oh no! So sorry about that issue. We're reaching out to you now to try and help."

Now, let's say my much better reply still doesn't appease Mr. Lawson because at this point, he's already missed the episode of American Idol he was trying to record. Pretend he replies with his same tweet that says, "*I write about TV for a living. I should be able to rely on the service I pay so much money for to work.*"

My responses to him would have been, *"You're right, and this is unacceptable. Look for a credit to your account next month!"* Then I would have emailed or called Mr. Lawson with a follow-up so he knew I took the matter seriously.

How do you think Mr. Lawson would have replied to that? Here's a big company acting like a not-so-big company—actually acting like a kind, thoughtful, *human being*. Not only does the customer get something out of this interaction, the company now has a reply on record that proves to anyone who sees it that they care about their customer's experience.

Removing humanity from the web is where we've started to go wrong. Customers want to connect with you on a human level, they don't just want slick automations. Yes, we want self-service any time we can get it. I'll be thrilled if I can find an answer in your help section without calling your customer service number! But what if I do need to interact with a human? Is a real person going to answer your phone number or am I going to scream into a phone tree for 15 minutes? If I tweet my frustrations will you reply quickly and offer to help, or will I get an automated cut-and-paste reply that doesn't resolve my problem and causes me even more frustration?

HOW CAN YOU BE MORE HUMAN WHEN ENGAGING WITH YOUR CUSTOMERS?

- Go the extra mile on behalf of your customers—don't ask them to do your job for you. Whenever you can, take the initiative to find customer info and track them down yourself to resolve a problem.
- People love to hear their own name, so reference customers *personally.*
- Whenever possible, offer to credit or refund customers for support issues. If they complain publicly, make sure you reply publicly *and* seek them out privately with a reply.
- If you're going to use scripted replies, make sure they sound genuine and personal.

- People are going to have temper tantrums on social media to get your attention. Remember that your replies are public and potentially seen by millions. Out of context, will your replies seem compassionate, helpful, friendly

SURPRISE & DELIGHT & REWARD & CELEBRATE

It's always bothered me when companies only give discounts to new customers. Sure, a discount for a new customer is great because they get to try your product without risk and maybe there's cool stuff in your app just for new customers, but what about the people that have already spent money on your products, or have been members for months or years? How do you show those customers that they're still valuable to you and that you appreciate their business?

A long time ago when I did support for a software company, I had the bright idea to send handwritten thank you notes to every single one of our customers. It was going to be my way of thanking them for signing up for an app and to let them know that there were *real people* out there that cared about them as customers. About 700 thank you letters later, I realized that was a really bad idea and my handwriting has never been the same since.

It was a great idea because it showed some initiative, but there were some better ways that I could have accomplished my goal. For one, I could have sent personal emails to every customer. If I wanted to be creepy, I could have called them all or driven to their house. (I did have their mailing address, I could have made a road trip out of it!) But then, I thought about how I would like to be recognized by a company for being a loyal customer. I realized the number one thing that I, as a loyal customer, really wanted or deserved was a credit or discount on the service I already paid for.

So, when my hand had permanently cramped and I had run out of notecards, I started crediting people's accounts for a month of service. When the credit was applied, I'd send a quick form email to let them know and thank them for being a customer. This was an igneous idea because it didn't cost me anything—I wasn't refunding money already spent by the customer or incurring any fees from credit card processors by involving their systems. I was simply buying our customers time and the opportunity to keep using our products. It took me about an hour each day to get through almost 4 years of our customer database over the course of 6 months.

I did more stunts like this while working for that company—sending thank you gift baskets to longtime customers who paid a certain dollar amount per month, contacting specific customers to highlight on our popular company blog, and mentioning others on our social media accounts.

And in the end, there was no difference to how customers responded to these perks. Customers who received a credit or a gift basket or a call or email all replied with gratitude and surprise.

Rewarding customers doesn't have to be extravagant or cost you actual cash. When you're giving credits to loyal customers for something they already happily pay for, a $10 credit goes a long way. An email doesn't cost you anything but your time, and that can be managed.

Here's how some forward-thinking companies are rewarding their customers:

- The support team at Sprout Social keeps an eye on high-profile customers over social media and sends them gift packages based on their interests. If you're a Sprout customer in Chicago, you may get some Intelligensia coffee delivered!
- Grubhub uses Snapchat to send surprise coupons to their followers, and lots of companies are dispensing coupon codes in their Instagram feeds. (Sure, Twitter and Facebook are good options, too, but they're kind of old hat by now, don't you think?)

However you decide to reward customers—whether it's real money, credit, or surprise discounts—make sure you're doing something fun and thoughtful that benefits *the customer*, not your company. You don't want to be a company that holds rewards hostage for survey responses or a certain number of shares. Real rewards are surprising and unconditional—make sure yours always are!

WHAT CAN YOU DO TO SHOW YOUR CUSTOMERS YOU CARE?

- Send handwritten notes! (Invest in a good pen and a stress ball!)
- Send personal notes or emails on customers' anniversaries using your app.
- Send personalized thank you notes to your first 100 customers who are still active.
- Profile customers and how they use your product on your blog or social media pages.
- Offer % discounts for customers after they pass the one year mark, and every anniversary after that.
- Follow top customers on social media and send them thank you gifts relevant to their interests (not company swag!)
- If you do send swag, make sure it's inclusive and fun. Who wants a corporate pen when you could send a beer koozie with your logo on it?
- Offer discounts for referrals, or set up an affiliate program that earns the customer account credit.
- Automatically pause billing on accounts that are inactive or dormant and contact the customer to let them know they won't be charged until they use it again.

- Are your customers local? Show up in person with a gift pack to introduce yourself! (Don't be creepy.)
- Include funny gifs or pictures in support emails when you have a good rapport with a customer.
- Post contests on your blog and offer account credits to anyone who participates (not just the winner!).
- Refund the last billing or credit accounts when a customer has had a frustrating support experience, even if they don't ask. (If they do ask, maybe give more than they ask for!)
- Hide discount or freebies in Instagram, SnapChat or other social feeds. (Yeah, we said SnapChat, but don't be creepy.)

"Anyone working for a big company might be skeptical that a large business, or even a strictly online business, can form the same kind of friendly, loyal relationship with customers as a local retailer. I'm saying it's already been done because I lived it."

— Gary Vaynerchuk

"Be helpful - even if there's no immediate profit in it."

— Susan War

BUILDING A TEAM OF LEADERS

BY JEFF VINCENT, DIRECTOR OF CUSTOMER HAPPINESS, *WISTIA*

"Customer Service" has to be one of the worst terms on the planet. When you tell your family or friends you work in Customer Service, they give you that look. You know the one. "Oh, so you work in a *call center*," is what their eyes are saying.

Let's face it, customer service isn't the sexiest function on any startup team. Much of our time is spent interfacing with customers who have never used a web application before, and we have the crazy email threads to prove it.

But there has been no function more important for the growth of our company than support. When our product was rough and incomplete, working closely with our customers was the only way we continued growing. As we've marched the product forward, support has informed us of the rough edges we didn't get right the first time, making our product more delightful and valuable to use.

Now that we have an established Customer Happiness team (five members strong), one of the things I spend most of my time thinking about is how to keep our team focused and motivated through the grind that is providing support.

At this point, we're doing a pretty okay job; our small team handles support for thousands of customers and has been consistently improving the customer experience.

But that won't come about automatically (or at least, it hasn't for me). It takes a lot of intentional work and focus to get it right. Over the last year, I've been focused on empowering our support team to act like leaders. They control a significant portion of the total customer experience, and empowering them to make decisions that impact that experience every day is the difference between a happy team of incredibly hard-working contributors, and a group of people looking for "the next opportunity."

To start, you must stop treating customer service as a place where creativity, uniqueness, and excitement go to die. Stop thinking of support as a bunch of inexperienced, unhappy people who should just glumly follow a script, day after day. Instead, involve your team in challenging work, and make sure their accomplishments are celebrated frequently.

Now, that sounds all well and good, but it's definitely not easy to implement. I'm not too proud to say that I've messed it up plenty of times. I want to tell you what I've learned from those mistakes, in the hopes you can avoid them completely.

ARTICULATE A CLEAR VISION

As team lead, it is my job to clearly lay out (and defend, and evolve) the company's vision for customer happiness. This vision has been developed carefully over time, and is driven by communicating with customers, internal discussion, and thinking deeply about the future of our business.

As we've grown, I have to remind myself to communicate this vision over and over again. There have been many, many times where I assumed my team understood my vision for customer service, instead of actually taking the time to communicate it.

Any goals we measure our support performance against (e.g., number of tickets, time to response, customer happiness rating) derive from our overarching vision. We don't spend much time worrying about the number of replies per conversation, for example, because changing that number doesn't get us any closer to achieving our end goals. Growth of total tickets relative to customer growth, however, is tracked closely, because we believe the best support is no support. The more customers who have a great experience and don't require a support conversation, the happier we hypothesize they'll be.

When the vision is clearly stated, and the connection between vision and performance measurement makes sense, my team can be fully empowered to make on-the-spot decisions. Situations that would go through a manager in other organizations can be pushed to the individual closest to the situation.

As an example, Jordan may spend an hour working through a common friction problem with developer Max, so that it can be resolved permanently. Jordan knows this may affect our time to reply, but he can make that trade-off because it gets us closer to achieving the overall vision.

As head of the team, make sure you create multiple venues to communicate your vision. I do my best to write it down, say it aloud again and again, and make it part of new team member on-boarding. Listen carefully to team feedback and defend your vision with reason and concrete examples, not with superiority.

During the hiring process, communicate the vision to potential candidates, and be ready to hire those that challenge your thinking. When you work with them to understand the vision, the right candidates will be excited to make it a reality.

FOSTER OWNERSHIP OVER KEY PROJECTS

Burnout is a huge risk for customer support team members. Handling hundreds of emails per week grates on the psyche and can wear down even the most gung-ho support person.

To combat this, make sure every member of the team is being challenged constantly and has other outlets for contributing to the team, beyond just the answering emails in the inbox. The first way we provide challenging work is through **ownership**.

Once a new team member is on-boarded and getting a handle on the key issues our customers face, I start a discussion with them about ownership, and specifically what they want to own within our team's purview.

We believe very strongly in ownership as a company—that having a point person to fight for projects they believe are important is the best way to make sure things get done well. No one gets to play dictator, but our output isn't a muddled mess, either.

Being able to run a specific project means they don't need my approval for making changes or taking risks. They get to **create** freely, which provides a great outlet for learning new things and contributing to our customers' overall joy in using the product.

In some cases, team members are going to pursue ownership over a project before you as team lead even think about it. This has never been a problem, as long as they continue to display mastery over their inbox work, which is their key responsibility. In other cases, team members might need more prodding to take on leadership roles in their own projects. This isn't necessarily a bad thing—there are many folks who are just happy to work as contributing team members. This is fine when all is going well, but I've found that distinct ownership can make it easier to fall back on something to contribute to when you are having an off-day or week.

When considering project ownership for team members to take on, I start by jotting down the team member's strongest talents, and some things that need work. I also solicit advice from the rest of the team—I ask them what this person loves to do or what parts of the customer's experience could really use their specific skill set.

Examples of ownership within our team are our onboarding webinar, our integration documentation, and our weekly inbox inventory email (which I talk about in further detail later).

DEVELOP PRODUCT SENSE

As a company, we are bombarded by feature requests—dozens every day. Most of them come through the support inbox. Most of these suggestions, frankly, are bad. To keep the product team from being inundated with these suggestions, it can seem like a totally great idea to create a rigid process for passing feature requests from the support team to product. Lots of organizations (ours included) have used spreadsheets, whiteboards, and other tracking tools to create an asynchronous sharing process (i.e., suggestions go somewhere for review at a later date).

Here are two disastrous side-effects of a rigid process like this: First, because of the cost incurred in logging and deciphering feature suggestions, no one will do it. This means product falls out-of-the-loop with requests from actual paying customers.

Second, a rigid process creates a shitty dynamic for support folks. They are getting all these requests, and they may not know what to do with them. They are not getting active, thorough feedback on the validity of feature suggestions. This can lead to zombie tickets, where no one knows how to respond to the request, so they just leave the email for someone else to clean up.

Make it a goal to develop a strong product sense in each and every member of your support team. This makes it easier to identify potentially valuable requests as they come in—no rigid process required. To start the process of building product sense, ensure everyone can receive near-immediate feedback for feature ideas and requests that come in through support. We talk about them as a team (in our chat room) and loop in the product team as appropriate.

By understanding the choices and thinking behind our product roadmap, each support team member gets trained as a product manager. They develop a filter that is strongly aligned with the product team, so that they can confidently respond to customer requests. This, of course, makes the support team member feel better, and it's a more positive experience for the customer as well.

CELEBRATE WINS

Spreading stories about the hard work Customer Happiness team members are putting in was a major challenge early on. It's really difficult to inspire folks from other disciplines when we talk about the number of emails answered or how this one conversation ended with a happy customer. *They just don't get us, man!*

We've been working to improve the communication between our team and the rest of the company, specifically finding ways to celebrate team wins. Two approaches we've found to be effective are consistent summary emails and public, centralized tracking of our out-of-the-inbox work.

Each week, we put together the inbox inventory, an email for the team with high-level support metrics. It contains metrics like volume of requests handled, response time, and the major issues from the week. This has inspired attention from the entire company on specific support problems, which leads to better and faster solutions. It is an incredible feeling to hear a member of the marketing team, for example, talking to a support team member about a big issue over lunch.

The second approach is placing our team roadmap in a centralized place. We've used Trello for this to great effect. When an issue comes in, we add it to our Customer Happiness Trello board. Typical issues for us are documentation confusion, places where our user experience could be improved, or ideas for new learning resources.

The team can comment on the issue, vote it up (great for establishing team priority), and pull in members from other teams as necessary. When the project is complete, having it documented already in a public place provides an excellent record of the achievement, which is huge for morale. This public record also makes it much easier for the rest of the company to celebrate these wins.

START EARLY

With everything else going on, it can seem unimportant to spend time deep thinking about your team members' motivation and leadership role in the company. Possibly something that can wait until years down the road. Please, take this advice from me: it is never too early to start.

I didn't think about this enough in the early years, and my first hires suffered as a result. It's been a tough "rip off the bandage" experience to get them where they could have been, had I done a better job. Set a strong vision for your team members, and then give them the tools and the power to drive your customer's experience forward. If you do that, you will find your team scaling support and customer joy far beyond what you could ever provide yourself

AMAZING PHONE SUPPORT MADE EASY

BY SHERVIN TALEIH, FOUNDER, DRUMBI

I hear this all the time from startups, emerging companies, and even Fortune 500 businesses: "We don't need to talk to our customers, they are happy with chat, email, or any one of our self-service options."

They continue by telling me that "phone calls don't scale. We can't figure out how to make it economical without affecting the customer's experience," and that agents really hate it too.

"Besides, all the young people prefer chat and Twitter. Why even bother with phones as an option for interacting with our customers?"

Wow. How did it come to this? How did we get to the point where our understanding of what people really want is so incredibly wrong? Turns out, most businesses don't really understand the nuanced change that is rapidly occurring in consumers, and how their interpretations are completely off.

HISTORY

Let's go back to 1844, the year when the first public telegraph was demonstrated. After the demonstration, it took a full twenty-two years before the first permanent telegraph cable was laid across the Atlantic Ocean. Want to know when email was invented? 1971. It wasn't for another full twenty years before it became a convention for business communications, and another five years before it fully hit its stride.

Throughout modern history, this twenty-year span from introduction to some semblance of popularity has been the norm for all innovative forms of communications.

UNTIL NOW

Over the past eight years, we have gone from zero to sixty, from introduction to widespread user adoption, with the advent of smartphones, tagging and sharing pictures, Facebook, Twitter, location-based apps, and a variety of messaging apps.

The results are remarkable. One in four people check their phones every five minutes; younger people do this even more frequently. We don't leave voicemails when calling friends or businesses. In fact, we send text messages and pre-arrange calls. We don't watch live television as often. While households are cutting the TV cord, video and rich content consumption is exploding.

We are increasingly shifting to asynchronous interactions, and when we must engage in synchronous interactions—like meeting face-to-face, going to a concert, or talking on the phone—we wrap this with many layers of asynchronous touches. For example, we share photos and videos while attending a live ball game or show. We start a phone call with, *"Wow. Your Instagram pictures of Portland were awesome. Looks like you had fun."* We no longer need to start each call with deep discovery, as so much of our context is available through apps, streams, and graphs.

So it's natural for businesses to want to invest in building great mobile apps, amazing websites, and mobile-optimized, web experiences. It's understandable that they would see the rise of asynchronous communications as a signal that people don't want to talk anymore.

That single false positive leads them to further ignore voice as a critical channel for prospects and customers and implement shortsighted solutions, like the dreaded phone-tree and automated attendant: *"Press 1 for Sales. Press 4 for Service. Enter your Account Number. Please hold."* Worse yet, many businesses even resort to hiding their phone number and even removing it altogether from their websites.

This is a colossal mistake.

Let's look at the typical "consideration" phase for consumers visiting a company's website when learning about a product or service the company provides. In a recent survey conducted between August and September of 2013, over 700 participants were asked, "*How important is it to have the option of calling a company when you are considering buying from them?*"

The results: 21% said it was very important; but even more staggering was that 31% stated that it was an absolute requirement. So if you decide to hide your phone number, making it harder for prospects to find it, or even remove it from your site, chances are that over 50% of your visitors will consider a competitor over your company as a result of this decision.

Let's look at another fallacy: If we offer chat, we don't need to offer phone calls. Using Google Consumer Surveys, between March and April of 2013, 200 people were asked to answer the following question: "*When using my mobile phone to contact a business for customer service, my preference is to a) speak to an agent, using voice, or b) chat, using text entry.*"

Over 71% preferred talking to someone. Why? While chat is a great experience on desktop and laptop form factors, it is not ideal for mobile and smartphones. Also, the proliferation of smartphones and high-speed, pervasive, online access has meant that people are increasingly on the go. Customer service through chat while driving, riding a bike, or walking to work isn't an ideal experience.

So what is the solution? What can we, as business owners, as heads of sales or customer service, do to give our customers what they want without losing margins?

Simply stated: **design a great experience for your customers, and all will be good.**

What does this mean? It means putting your customer at the center of your customer experience design. It means having a deep understanding of what they really want, and how to provide it for them.

When it comes to phones, this also means avoiding some of the most annoying and, unfortunately, most popular techniques used by businesses today. When asked, "*What business practice would make you consider a different vendor?*" respondents stated the following:

- Scripted greetings (having your agents read out a highly structured greeting and engagement script): 31%
- Hiding your phone number: 21%
- Asking for detailed contact information ("what is your name, account number, email") before helping them: 20%

"But," you say, *"I must have a structured script. I must ask for detailed contact information. How else can I help the customer? How else can I update my systems?"*

What if I told you that your attempt to "help" your prospect or customer and the process you have created are actually hurting you, and that it doesn't need to be this way.

I have learned this from my wife, and from many other personal events that anyone can relate to. Here are a few lessons I've learned worthy of being shared on this subject:

FIRST LESSON: BEFORE YOU TALK, LISTEN

I remember watching Sports Center on TV as my wife talked to me. Every ten or fifteen seconds, to indicate I was listening to her I would say, *"Really? Okay. Wow. That's interesting."* In fact, I would quickly try to offer my "fix" or remedy for any situation she brought up, trying to shorten the conversation and thinking that I was actually being helpful. If she would stop me and ask, *"What did I just say?"* I would successfully repeat the key points she made during the past few minutes.

But she would stop me and say, *"You're listening to me, but I am not being heard."*

What my wife wanted from me in those moments is exactly what your customers want when they contact you: to be heard. Instead of quickly trying to solve their problem or run them through a scripted process, we should simply say, *"Hello, how can I help you?"* or *"My name is Shervin. Tell me, how you are doing?"*

And then the best thing to do is to just let them talk. Let them share their feelings. Let them tell you their story. Don't force them to go through your sequence, like giving you an account number first; just let them tell you exactly how they are feeling. When we give people the opportunity to speak, and we show them that we are actually focused on what they are saying, then we can relate to how they are feeling and show that we have empathy for them. Empathy is at the core of understanding. Empathy doesn't entail that "100% guarantee that I can fix your problem!" I would argue empathy is even better than that. It sets the tone for an honest discussion, whereby the customers know they will be heard. By simply listening to our customers and not necessarily solving their problem 100% of the time on the spot, we can create a completely different type of relationship with them.

SECOND LESSON: DON'T SHOW UP AND THROW UP

Do you remember going on a really great first date? Rather than talking a ton about yourself, you instead focused on getting to know your companion. You did this by first asking a few questions, then sharing a bit about yourself, and back and forth until pretty soon you were having a real conversation.

Compare this to how you handled yourself when you first started dating. You would perpetually over-talk, have little or no curiosity about really getting to know your date, and do what I call "show up and throw up."

This isn't the basis for great relationships, and we shouldn't start a business interaction this way either.

Instead of peppering our callers with questions or hammering them with a script, we should remember how great conversations work: ask a question and then listen, share a little and then ask a little, and most importantly listen. Make your customers feel like they are at the center of your universe. *It works!*

FINAL LESSON: BE AUTHENTIC

I remember hearing a story from a good friend of mine. She had been single for a while and had turned to various dating sites hoping to meet Mr. Right. She told me that when she first signed up, she found lots of great profiles, guys that almost sounded too good to be true. So she packed a weekend with a bunch of first dates, expecting to find true love in any one of these encounters.

Well, it didn't turn out that way. In fact, all of the guys she met were nothing like their profiles. To start with, they all lied or greatly exaggerated their physical features, like their height and weight. Most of them were nowhere near as professionally accomplished as their profiles made them out to be either. This created a really odd first few moments in the relationship: "You are not the person you made me think you would be, so how do I know if anything you do or say is true?"

This is precisely what happens when we call a company and speak with someone overseas. To start with, they are given some common American name and a heavily scripted introduction. It's not that we hate dealing with offshore call centers, it's that we hate being lied to, and I know your name isn't Bob. I don't hate you, Bob, I hate the company that is forcing you to change your name and have you deny who you are, where you are from, or who I am actually talking to. It starts our relationship off with a set of lies, and that just isn't a good recipe for building trust.

Incidentally, authenticity is not the same as not telling a lie. Being truthful is part of being authentic, but to truly be authentic you need to reveal context: who you are, where you're from, how you feel, and what makes you unique.

This is why we prefer mom-and-pop restaurants, owned and operated by first-generation immigrants. The recipes aren't based on some book; it's what their grandmothers made for them. They don't pretend to be someone else and would prefer to share what they know and who they are with you, their guest.

PUTTING IT ALL TOGETHER

So just how do you provide an amazing phone experience for your customers? Hire great people (never make your customers leave voice-mail!), give them access to a phone solution that works (for them AND your callers!), empower them to do the right thing (no phone scripts!), and trash every single "industry standard metric" for running your call center. Not only do these measures not work, they have really bad unintended consequences (ever wonder why you are getting transferred 5 times or asked to answer a stupid survey after every call or email interaction?).

Simply stated again: Design an experience that is human, for your customers AND your people, and all will be good!

"A lot of people have fancy things to say about customer service, but it's just a day-in, day-out, ongoing, never-ending, persevering, compassionate kind of activity."

— *Christopher McCormic*

CREATING A SUPPORT TEAM CULTURE THAT THRIVES

BY LAURA GLUHANICH, FOUNDER, *SIGNAL CAMP*

The word "culture" has become a catchphrase, seeming to mean beer kegs, ping pong tables and free massages provided by a company in exchange for your working an inappropriate number of hours. But culture is something built from the bottom up by an entire team, subconsciously. It's how a team embodies and displays their values. Companies can foster a thriving culture by getting out of the way, providing the space and resources for culture to flourish, and supporting efforts that directly speak to team values.

So, the questions to start with are:

- What are your values?
- How do you envision those values playing out in your team?
- How can you measure whether they are being thought of in larger projects and day to day?

All this brainstorming will take an hour or two of discussions as a team, documenting *how* you want to operate and what you want to stand for within your company, for your users, and as a product. Create a document that is accessible to all, and revisit it regularly to ensure your values align with what you are doing. If they don't, either change what you are focusing on, or change your stated values.

START WITH FUN THINGS

When I worked at Ning, our community team acquired a stuffed dog we named Puggins McGee. I don't even know where he came from—perhaps a white elephant gift party? Each week at standup, someone was awarded Puggins for going above and beyond with a customer, teammate, or somewhere else in our support structure. The Puggins Gifter was the previous week's Puggins Giftee.

Puggins became a fun part of our culture and also encouraged recognizing great work that supported our team values and goals. At some point, each subsequent Puggins Giftee started adding accessories to him—a tiara, button, mp3 player, earrings. It got weird, but super fun and creative, ending with one of the fanciest stuffed dogs to ever grace Palo Alto.

We also had a cardboard fireplace that moved offices a few times with us. The fireplace didn't really embody any value but it was decorated regularly and was a nice way for our team to claim ownership of a place in the office. Silly? Sure. Did it represent the personality of our community team? You bet.

We did other things as a team to get us out of the office regularly: a visit to a popup Lego museum, Go-Kart racing, park cleanup or food bank volunteering, and even group ski trips. Not every team member did every activity, and that was good. Nothing felt *forced*—you could participate where and when you wanted. But if you didn't it was ok; as long as you put in the work to be part of the team, you were respected.

HIRE FOR CULTURE

Puggins and a cardboard fireplace sitting in the office set a tone for our team and for potential hires. Hiring for culture is totally *a legit thing* but it should be broad, not prescriptive. It shouldn't matter if someone likes baseball, but do they support recognizing great work in people they work next to? Hiring for culture is less about having similar personal hobbies and interests and more about having similar personal values.

It's important to outline your company or team values so you hire people aligned with them. It doesn't help to just ask if they agree with your values verbatim. Figure out ways you can determine they jibe with what you value. In interviews with potential hires we'd try to uncover something that the person is passionate about—how do they talk about it? Do they get us excited about it? Can they articulate why they love it?

We also looked for people specifically motivated by *helping others.* Do strangers randomly ask them for directions, for example? Do they speak highly of collaborative experiences rather than competitive ones?

Of course with a smaller team—let's say a team of one—hiring for culture is pretty low on the totem pole. But I'd argue it's even more important that your partner in work shares the values and priorities that you do.

I'm currently the cofounder of a two-person company and the most important thing we did when founding our company was talk about it for about *six months before doing any work.* We discussed what we wanted to accomplish personally and professionally, who we wanted to work with, and the kind of life that is important for us.

Beyond that, to keep yourself sane, hire a counterpart whose strengths pair well with your weaknesses. Whether it's communicating about money, building slide decks, or writing blog posts, having a second person who can fill the gaps in your skills will make your life immensely better.

HAVE A CELEBRATION CULTURE!

My co-founder and I just celebrated our two year (business) anniversary. One of the best things we've done is really focus on communication and celebrating. We've had dinner celebrations a couple times a year, all at the same restaurant, celebrating things like our first paycheck, or renewing our domain for another year. This is now "our" restaurant, and they recently offered us a complimentary dessert in honor of our anniversary, perpetuating our celebration and support of one another.

In both my current team and the best teams I've participated in, verbalizing appreciation regularly set a great tone for communication and culture. From passing around a Puggins to offering an explicit "I appreciate you" IM, these shows of recognition spill goodwill into other parts of your life and make it more enjoyable.

Don't forget to celebrate user and customer milestones with the entire team. If a Ning Network Creator posted about a membership or engagement goal they reached, the entire team would congratulate them. The team I worked with at about.me would send an annual summary of milestones by the community and celebrate some of the most popular pages the last week of the year in a series of blog posts. Get the whole community involved in celebrating themselves!

Do the same for team members. Track important life events like birthdays and anniversaries with the company. Send out an email, mention it in chat or post it to your social networks. I consider it a testament to the team at Ning that so many have gone on vacations together and been in each other's weddings.

Culture is reflected in the work you do and the experience your users have with your team and product. It's important to be intentional with them, as what you put out as a team will come back in spades with the community you build.

"If we can keep our competitors focused on us while we stay focused on the customer, ultimately we'll turn out all right."

— Jeff Bezos

"Your most unhappy customers are your greatest source of learning."

— Bill Gates

HELP DOCUMENTS ARE FOR PEOPLE

BY JASON REHMUS, FOUNDER, *SWEATING COMMAS*

Despite working on a team that pushes pixels and wrangles bits, you're in the people business. People use your app. People often don't understand how your software works. People need help from time to time.

Making those people happy ensures they keep using your app, but it doesn't have to require a huge daily time investment. Do the work of writing good help documentation once, and make your customers happy over and over again.

GOOD FOR YOU

Good help documents make your customers happy, but they'll make you and your team happy, too. When people are able to answer their own questions, they don't need to write in or call you for help. Your team can focus on the work that moves your product forward, instead of scrambling to explain how some basic feature works. Replying to fewer emails means less distraction for everyone on your team.

Not only do they reduce distraction, well-written help documents provide a way to repeatedly impress your customers. Every interaction with a customer is a chance to share your company's values, the reason you exist. When the language you use in your documents reflects this, you strengthen the bond between you and your customer, building trust and earning respect.

GOOD FOR YOUR CUSTOMERS

The benefits for your customer, though, are the real reason to invest time in excellent supporting documentation for your app. Beyond simple clarifications, your documents can provide a sense of accomplishment to those people who help themselves and can even open their eyes to features they didn't know about.

Your help documents are always available to your customers. Support teams need to sleep, help desk agents take lunch and coffee breaks, but your documents are always right there when help is required. Being able to find an answer as soon as a question comes up is priceless to customers. They're already frustrated by the problem they've encountered. Providing the answer to them in your documents alleviates that frustration and allows your customers to get back to their work. They won't need to waste time trying to "fix" your app, or waiting for a reply to their email or phone call.

If you've taken the time to organize your help articles into logical categories, your customers can proactively learn about unfamiliar features while they're searching for the help they need. In this way your documents become more than just a set of quick answers. They can be a rich source of training for your customers, leading them to use your app even more.

The self-service mindset can also benefit customers in ways that only indirectly involve your app. They'll get a sense of achievement from finding an answer on their own or learning something new without help. They had a problem that they solved by themselves, or maybe they discovered something new that helps them a lot, and now they feel good. Not only can customers feel good about solving their own problems, they can become the expert on their team. Your help documents empower your customers to help others, scaling your goodwill.

We're all different. Some people like to figure out how to use an app on their own. Others want a phone call and some patient assistance before they're comfortable trying something new. When a customer reaches out to you, they're already desperate for help. If they get to the point where they need to write in to ask a question, that means they've tried everything else. Well-written and clear documents can be the hand holding your customer wants. Write the documents once, and hold your customer's hands every day.

OH SHE REAL MAD

I read something the other day in an article about customer service that seemed odd to me: *"Studies show that the vast majority of unsatisfied customers will never come right out and tell you they're unsatisfied."*

I don't know which unsatisfied customers this author was thinking of, but the ones I know aren't the type to keep things to themselves. And I have to admit, when *I* am the unsatisfied customer in question, the very first thing I want to do is TELL THE WHOLE WORLD.

We live in an age of *immediate* complaint, where everyone has several outlets to express their gripes and grumbles. There's the old standby, Facebook, where the Average Joe can moan about the time it's taking for an oil change or the last-minute cancellation of a Zumba class, only after expensive childcare was procured. There's Yelp and TripAdvisor which all but encourage bitchy—sorry, *honest*—reviews of any company, regardless of the effect those reviews may have or how ridiculous they may be. I once read a Yelp review about a well-known chicken and waffles joint that read, *"I'm not big into chicken or waffles. One star."* Here's an idea: *Don't go to a place with the words* ***chicken*** *or* ***waffles*** *in its name.*

And then there's Twitter. Mecca for the complainers, Zion for the dissatisfied, Utopia for the unfulfilled. A constant stream of timestamped complaints rolling along uncontrollably, some potentially attached to our names for eternity. Twitter is like Wonderland for angry customers who want to tweet before they think.

If we're going to talk about irate customers, I can't think of anywhere to start than with myself. I am the absolute worst person on the planet to have a bad customer experience with because I am often unrelenting when it comes to my expectations of service. And sometimes—I'm sure you can't believe this—I am a jerk about it on Twitter. Yes, even me, Miss Customer Service Maven, advocate to the poor souls manning the phones, empathizer to the interns stuck replying on Twitter. If pushed to my limit, even I can be a whiny, melodramatic mess in 140 characters or less.

A while back I was traveling home from Palm Springs when my flight was canceled. Being stuck in Palm Springs wouldn't have mattered much had it not been a torrential downpour that caused flash flooding and the cancellation of all flights for over 24 hours. I decided to use a newish app called Hotel Tonight that exists to find you a hotel, like, *tonight*. It's fantastic for desperate travelers or adventurous bargain hunters since it actually only books you a hotel ... *tonight*!

So, there I was booking myself a hotel because I was trapped in my anti-paradise, entirely annoyed that I wouldn't be home in my own bed after weeks of traveling. I opened the app, found a room close by, paid for it and hopped in a cab. When I got to the hotel to check in to my hotel for tonight, the desk clerk said those words you never want to hear: *"We don't seem to have a reservation for you."*

"But," I protested, *"I **just** paid for it! Look—it's right here in the app!"*

The desk clerk checked the app then said, *"Ohhhh, yeah. They sell our rooms but we don't have a way to access those reservations. We don't know why they do that."*

I just stood there, soaking wet in the lobby of a 5-star hotel, *seething with rage.* I called Hotel Tonight and didn't have a great interaction with their team over the phone. First it was the hotel's fault, then it was the app's fault, then it was my fault, and then it was the hotel's fault. With every passing of the buck my privileged and impatient blood boiled higher! Eventually, they promised they'd figure things out and call me back, but never explained whether or not I'd actually get my room.

And then I went to Twitter.

Now, I know I shouldn't have done what I did, but we all fail in our humanity sometimes, don't we? Something about the space between our avatars makes it easy to behave as less rational human beings when we're clicking away our reviews and thumbs-down.

I could have just waited for the call back from Hotel Tonight and worked on my stress reduction meditation techniques, but instead I chose to call them out on Twitter in front of 40k+ followers:

> *"Flight canceled. Booked a @HotelTonight. Hotel doesn't have paid reservation on file. HT customer support = atrocious.* ***Send wine.****"*

It's not really a bad tweet, in fact it's way nicer than some other complaints I saw, and Hotel Tonight replied pretty nicely considering:

> *"@sh We apologize for the inconvenience. Now that you're all checked-in, please don't hesitate to call us if we can help w/ anything else."*

And here's where I turned into a total jerk:

> *"@HotelTonight & I won't be calling- I learned today I can't trust your service as a customer & that's a bummer."*

With that, imagine me thrusting on my oversized sunglasses and whipping my feathered boa around my neck as I stormed off. *I said good day, sir!*

I look back on this interaction and I cringe, thinking not just about my horrendous behavior but how that must have felt to the person running Hotel Tonight's Twitter account who was clearly trying to help. Often when we're Yelping and Facebooking our disappointment we aren't thinking of the person who's reading those complaints and wants to fix things for us. We're thinking of ourselves and our immediate dissatisfaction, and we're looking for someone out there to blame for it.

I want to share this story not just to acknowledge the perilous world of social media and my own emotional instability when I'm traveling, but because Hotel Tonight recovered from this situation in a startling way.

Not too long after I finally got my hotel room, I received a personal email from Hotel Tonight's support manager:

> *"Hey Sarah,*
>
> *I just wanted to take a moment and apologize for what happened during your call to our support team today. The level of support we offer and the personal connections we make with our travelers is something we take great pride in here. After reviewing your experience, it's clear that we missed the mark when working with you today. We were able to assist the Riviera to get your booking into their system, but it took some time and we have yet to offer you a heartfelt apology. We know we can do better. I can say this confidently because 9 times out of 10, we do. So, on behalf of my team, I'm truly sorry.*
>
> *That said, there's always room to improve our service and that's something that our team is working on every day. I'd love the chance to connect with you to chat about your experience both with HT and as a profes-*

sional. Tonight and any time, please feel free to reach out to me directly."

Wow. That is an *awesome* email. What a sincere apology! I was absolutely flabbergasted by this email, which goes to show that any bad customer interaction—no matter how melodramatic—can be turned around with a little bit of human touch. Just as I was tweeting about this amazing gesture, there was a knock on my hotel room door. I'd received a delivery from the Hotel Tonight team: that bottle of wine I'd so desperately *whined* about needing and another note of apology for me.

I have to admit, I was stunned at this gesture from Hotel Tonight, and immediately took to Twitter and Instagram to express how they'd righted the situation for me. I even apologized for my own social media temper tantrum, which is the true sign a company has really done an amazing job of recovering.

What went wrong in my situation is clear: The app didn't work as expected, phone support didn't resolve the problem as expected, and the language used wasn't very personal. **But what went right is what actually matters:**

- The email from the support manager used a friendly opener and not a stock "professional" greeting
- Hotel Tonight acknowledged their failures and offered sincere regret for the situation

- The apology was truly heartfelt — I didn't doubt for a moment that it was genuine
- Hotel Tonight followed up the apology with *another apology*!
- And they sent an appropriate gift!
- Holy crap!

When it comes to situations like this, the goal here is simple: If a customer complains publicly—no matter how ridiculous, spoiled, or rude they are—our job should be to turn their experience around. We should focus on *fixing* their experience with us so their original complaint isn't the last thing they remember. Even if a bad situation becomes a story they tell their friends or write about melodramatically in books, you have the advantage if the end chapter revolves around your incredible, personal, intentional recovery.

A few months after my first bad Hotel Tonight experience, I used their app when I was once again stranded during travels. Within hours of booking, I got an email from their support team welcoming me back, and thanking me for giving them another chance. I stood in a crowded airport taxi queue reading the email on my phone, and had the immediate urge to tell every single person near me what an amazing experience using their app had been.

* *http://www.entrepreneur.com/article/65768*

"Customers don't expect you to be perfect. They DO expect you to fix things when they go wrong."

— Donald Porter

MEASURING REAL HAPPINESS

The idea of "customer happiness" is a big new buzz term in support these days. Many CEOs and marketing managers who've never replied to a support email in their life think that the most important thing about their customer support is a smiley face rating or a thumbs-up vote from a customer. But as support professionals (people who do this day in and day out) we know there's a lot more to keeping customers happy than just doing and saying things that will get you a good review.

Don't get me wrong. Those ratings can be awesome, and from a high level perspective it's really helpful to see trends and patterns around your support structure. The problem is these ratings are often an emotional response a customer has to a specific event in time or a specific interaction and isn't necessarily indicative of overall "happiness."

A few years ago I worked for a tech company that wanted to determine whether their customer support was "successful" and if customers were "happy." A system was integrated that allowed customers to rate our support emails without prejudice. Let's say we didn't offer a feature the customer wanted. They just had to vote that our response was BAD to voice their opinion. If a customer didn't like us saying *"Hi"* instead of *"Hello,"* they could rate our reply poorly and we'd be held accountable for that. The endgame for this seemed simple enough: The more poor responses meant that support person was doing a bad job and customers were unhappy.

Think of when you've been asked to rate your experience as a customer, perhaps when you're handed a 2-foot long receipt for a pack of gum you just bought. It's a purely emotional event: You're either overwhelmed with joy because the person was so fast and friendly, or you're annoyed because they wasted your time and gave you a bunch of trash to deal with. How is your filling out a survey in any way an accurate depiction of your overall "happiness"? It's not and it never can be. Likewise, those email ratings you request from customers are only a small, small portion of what you should be considering when you want to look to see who's happy and why.

When you choose to tell your support team that it's more important for you to see Red, Yellow, or Green next to their name, you rob them of the joy of being part of your product development. Instead, you throw back on them this idea that they're on constant alert to just answer fast, smooth things over, and make everyone's emotions about your product positive, regardless of sincerity. They're not there for any other reason when you equate their entire day's work to a thumbs up icon.

Instead, the leader of a great support team demands excellence in a much more practical way: by asking support agents what customers are feeling, what customers are saying, what customers need, and what customers really want. When your support team presents to you a case for changing a feature, it's based on their experience with multiple customers and that particular feature. If your reply is, *"I don't get that problem,"* or *"We designed it that way for a reason,"* it sounds like you care more about your design philosophy and ego than the "happiness" of people paying you money for a product.

Customer happiness isn't really about support emails, and it's not about whether a customer got a timely retweet from your community managers. Customers express their real emotions around your product and features, and that's what you should be tracking.

Here are some practical ways you can accurately measure customer happiness or their feelings about your product:

- **Use the words your customers use in their emails to your team to gauge their emotions using your product.** Not just whether they liked your support agent. Not just if they said, *"Thanks!"* Measure based on words they use such as love, hate, annoying, doesn't have, need, want. Split these into "happy" or "unhappy" categories and use tags or labels in your help desk to track the levels monthly.

- **Keep track of customers' feelings on new features and take it back to the designer.** Your designers are making choices that affect customers, so let's hold them responsible. Your customer support team is your first line of defense for customers complaining about new features, and they rarely get a chance to chime in with their design or development ideas. When it comes to new features, work with your support team to track percentages of love vs. hate to know when you need to change or modify a design.
- **Measure speed of reply by your agents.** You don't even need your customers to tell you, "Thanks for the fast response," when you see the average responses time is 30 minutes. Is it over an hour? That's something to work on. Most help desk apps will tell you this information, and it should be the responsibility of your support manager to keep tabs on response times.
- **Track number of support requests vs. number of active customers.** Do the math. If 25% of your users need to write support each month, something is wrong. If it's even more than that, it's time to make your product more usable: improve your help section, add more online tutorials, increase in-app help, and offer training webinars or Google hangouts for new customers.

Real customer happiness is a mix of things, and never just one or the other. If you're thinking that customer support "success" and "happiness" can be measured with emoticons, you'll never have a true representation of what your customers really like, really want, and really need from your team.

It's the job of a product manager or startup founder to listen intently to your support agents. Unless you're answering 80% of the support emails yourself, you have zero idea what customers are really asking or complaining about. Your support team knows, and if they're good at their job, they're keeping track of the general feeling customers have about new features, old features, lack of features, whatever. They may even keep lists or track tags of the top requests—data that the product developer needs to make your product better.

If happiness is what you want to track, stop rating *just* customer responses to support emails and start rating their responses to specific *features*. Each time someone emails about feature X, tag that email so it cross-references their rating of your support agent. You'll start building actual customer responses on issues instead of just emotional reactions to particular people or situations.

FINDING YOUR SUPPORT VOICE

Without being too dramatic, the words you choose to use when speaking to your customers can make or break the relationship. Words can make you look like a lifeless robot typing out meaningless words with no empathy, or they can endear you to a customer when they see that you're a real human being who really cares about their experience.

But your words can also be way more powerful if you *find your voice*, which is just a fancy way of saying that what you write sounds like what **you** would say in a normal conversation. Not your boss, or your lawyer, but *you*. Too often, we think we need to sound "professional" or buttoned down in our communication with customers, but we're learning that 21st-century customers really don't want that. They don't want companies hiding behind legalese or technical jargon, or using boilerplate corporate phrases.

Customers value informal conversation over corporate-speak any day, and companies who are "winning" in the eyes of the customer are consistently keeping things casual. And by *casual*, I don't mean you start calling every customer "Dude" or pepper all your correspondence with emojis. But it does mean experimenting with how your words come across in print and how that relates to your corporate brand. If your company is known for being quirky, fun, and informal, the words you choose to use with customers should reflect that.

Here are some of the easiest ways to break through your bland and impersonal daily communication and find the true voice of your support team:

- **Use proprietary words and phrases to brand your support experience.** Marketing teams have been doing this for years, and for the most part, it works really well. I once worked with a company who had very specific words they used when referring to their customer support process. For instance, they told me, *"We don't call them 'help articles,' we call them 'resources.'"* They felt that tagging "help" onto anything automatically made it sound complicated and scary, so they chose to use educational terms. You don't have to go all out in renaming every facet of your system, but consider changing the job title of your support agents, or referring to your support system in words specific to your brand.
- **Emulate your work environment.** What's it like going to work everyday and talking with your coworkers? Do you converse around ping pong tables and bean bag chairs? Think of how you would greet a coworker or explain something to them if they came to you in person to ask a question. Most like-

ly, you wouldn't use "professional" phrases, you'd break things down in a more informal and easy going tone. If you work from home, think about your home life, your friends and family. How would you answer a question a friend posed over dinner?

- **Use contractions and exclamation points!!!** I know, it's scary to think about, isn't it? You don't want to come off as a peppy sorority girl, nor do you want to look like a sloppy writer. If you're writing the next great American novel, it may be ok to use cannot, will not, and should not. But in email correspondence, especially to strangers, it comes off as harsh and a bit caustic. Using contractions instead helps to lighten the mood of your written conversation, and adding exclamation points to key phrases also helps to brighten your tone. You don't have to use exclamation points for every sentence, but consider using them for your first greetings and to close emails with customers. (e.g., *"Hi Robert!"* and *"Let me know if you need anything else!"*)
- **Read your email out loud.** If you're wondering what your support voice sounds like, try listening to your actual voice. Hearing your written words spoken will give you insight into how your customers are reading those same words, and help you soften or tighten up your language.

Here are some quick examples of replacing robotic language with more human-sounding words:

OPENING STATEMENTS

All emails should start with a friendly acknowledgment of the customer's name. Try using "*Hi*" instead of "*Hello,*" and make sure the customer knows in your opening that you're there to help.

Sample replies:

- *"Hi Mark! Thanks for getting in touch!"*
- *"Hi Cindy, I'd love to help you out with this."*
- *"Hey Tyler, Sorry to hear you're having this issue!"*

CLOSING STATEMENTS

When you close an email, always thank the customer for getting in touch and offer to help more if needed. Offer to answer more questions and allow the conversation to continue. **Pro Tip:** Include a link to your online help section or forum in your footer script so your customers can keep finding more educational info on your product.

Sample replies:

- *"Thanks again for contacting support!"*
- *"Let us know if you need anything else."*
- *"Hope that solves all your problems. We're always here to help!"*

RESPONSES FOR TROUBLESHOOTING AN ISSUE

Anytime a person reports a problem, a first response to them should be to apologize for the trouble and let them know you're going to fix it. Here are some examples of a first response to a trouble ticket:

- *"Sorry to hear you're having this issue! Let me help you get this sorted out."*
- *"Sorry about that trouble. We can definitely help you with this."*
- *"I'm sorry you ran into that issue! If I can get some more info from you, we can get you a quick fix."*

ASKING FOR MORE INFO

When you need more information from a person, the most important thing is that they know why you're asking for it. Sometimes going back and forth with more info can be frustrating for a customer, so let them know it's important to get the facts before troubleshooting starts. After you've acknowledged and apologized for the issue, you'll want to request more information like this:

- *"We'll be happy to help troubleshoot it for you, but first we'll need some more details."*
- *"I think I know what the issue may be, but getting some more information from you will help me know for sure."*

- *"It sounds like you're hitting a bug we're aware of, so I need to gather some more info from you to be sure and get that fixed for you."*

RESPONSES FOR LINKING TO THE SUPPORT CENTER

When you're sending out links to the Help site, make sure to offer a summary of the answer, and then clearly link to the section in Help.

- *"Here's more information about that from our help center ..."*
- *"You can find more help for issues like this in our online Knowledge Base."*
- *"We've written up a detailed overview of this in our Help section ..."*

BEST PRACTICES

"A brand not responding on Twitter is like hanging up the phone on customers with millions watching."

— Dave Kerpen

"When you're trying to make an important decision, and you're sort of divided on the issue, ask yourself: If the customer were here, what would she say?"

— Dharmesh Shah

APOLOGIZING

Question: *"If something goes wrong, what's the best way to convince a customer we're really sorry and keep them from going nuts on Twitter?"*

Answer: Seriously? Just say you're sorry!

Back when you were a kid and you'd do something bad, your parent or teacher would instruct you to apologize. We've all muttered a sheepish, *"Sorry,"* under our breath in our lifetime, and we've all heard someone admonish us, *"Say it like you mean it!"*

The number one thing most companies get wrong is apologizing to customers, either publicly or privately. Especially when it comes to large legacy brands, style guides often dictate exactly what agents and customer service reps must say in crisis conditions. If you're working under one of those guidelines, tear the next few pages out of this book, photocopy it a few hundred times, and make sure it gets in front of whomever approves that style guide you have to use.

We've known since we were kids that there's a difference between saying the word and expressing a sincere regret that a situation has occurred. Using that same logic when it comes to our customer's experiences ensures that our communication around all bad events is intentional and empathetic. There are three main qualities any apology has to have in order to be taken seriously:

- You have to apologize to your customers like you mean it, as you would like to be apologized to if someone had really let you down.
- You have to be clear and friendly with your responses.
- You have to communicate that you're working on a solution or have one already.

Customers want to be heard. They want you to take responsibility. They want you to fix it. Here are three scenarios we will all encounter at one point that will require a sincere apology, along with examples of what to say.

SCENARIO #1: WHEN A CUSTOMER'S HAD A BAD EXPERIENCE.

Any bad experience—even those that seem trivial—can make or break your relationship with a customer. How you reply to those experiences will determine if the customer sees you as authentic, engaged, and concerned about their happiness. The language you choose to use with customers can turn any bad experience around if it's sincere and helpful.

Remember: In cases where customers may be complaining on social media or public forums, your responses are a historical record of how your company believes customers should be treated. Choose your words wisely!

Instead of "I apologize," **say**, *"I'm really sorry."*

Instead of "We're sorry for the inconvenience," **say,** *"I understand your frustration and I'm very sorry this happened."*

Instead of "I'm sorry for this issue," **say,** *"I'm sorry for this hassle."*

Sample replies:

- *"You're right, we could definitely do this better."*
- *"Thanks for being open and honest about your experience so we can learn from it."*
- *"I really appreciate your helping us improve our process—we don't want this to happen again."*

SCENARIO #2: YOUR PRODUCT GOES DOWN OR HAS A BUG THAT'S CAUSED AN ISSUE FOR A CUSTOMER.

Anything related to downtime or an app not functioning properly needs to be escalated to top priority. Reply **FIRST** on social media, explaining that you're aware of and working on the issue. Next, tackle all emails with a similar response, and include links to your social media accounts so customers and follow along and keep informed of progress. ***(See the next chapter on Downtime for more help with this!)***

Once the issue is fixed, every customer who reported a bug or downtime should be sent a followup email the next day, extending more apologies and encouraging them to try again. If you're *really* diligent and committed, use tags and filters to track all emails related to the issue, then follow up again with those customers one month out.

Instead of "We're currently assessing the issue," **say,** *"We're looking into what went wrong and will get back to you soon with more info."*

Instead of "We're aware of this issue," **say**, *"We're working on this right now and hope to have it fixed very soon."*

Instead of "We appreciate your patience," **say,** *"Thanks so much for bearing with us while we fix this!"*

Sample replies:

- *"I know this is a huge disruption to your day and I'm working to get it fixed."*
- *"I'm so sorry for this downtime! Our whole team has jumped in to fix the issue and get everyone back online."*

SCENARIO #3: WHEN IT'S THE CUSTOMER'S FAULT!

This is going to happen. Trust me. A customer will forget to cancel an account and still be billed, or they will try and add javascript to a text field and break everything. It will happen. Once, when I was working on an app that included a web-based calendar, a customer tried to set a daily recurring reminder for the next 275 years and overloaded the entire app. (His very important, multi-centennial reminder that crashed the system was the phrase, *"Eat a snack."*)

The important thing to remember is that even if it is the customer's fault, your response should still cushion the fall. Customers have their own responsibility when using products, and that's not something that should be ignored, but there doesn't need to be a fight for blame when you're working out a solution to a problem.

Instead of "This isn't our fault," **say**, *"It doesn't appear that an issue in our system caused this."*

Instead of *"This looks like an issue you caused,"* **say,** *"I'm not sure this is a system issue, but I can still help with it."*

Sample replies:

- *"I'm really sorry you ran into this trouble! It looks like the problem was ..."*
- *"Thanks for letting me look into this for you. Here's what I've found so far ..."*

DOWNTIME

Question: *"How should we communicate with customers if there's serious downtime or if our app is hacked?"*

Answer: Communicate everything, constantly, then communicate more!

Downtime, malicious bugs, hacking—anyone working with the web knows these are all things that are bound to happen. It happens to Facebook, it happens to Gmail, and your life in customer support will be much easier if you just accept the fact that it will happen to you. Being prepared before a crisis hits can be your triumphant recourse and save your company's reputation, despite whatever trouble you go through.

WHEN YOU'RE IN THE MIDDLE OF IT:

Immediately jump on social media and announce the issue to everyone. You may not have time or resources to reply to every customer, yet, but getting the word out as quickly as possible shows you're aware of the issue and are acknowledging it.

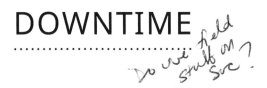

Next, triage emails and start replying to customers over email or chat. It's ok if you don't have a fix yet, what matters is that you are *responsive* in their time of need. It's a good idea to script out a few phrases you can use in template emails or copy and paste to make replying faster, but make sure that anything you say is human, sincere, and informative. Keep these rules in mind when writing your scripted replies:

Instead of "We're currently assessing the issue," **say,** *"We're looking into what went wrong and will get back to you soon with more info."*

Instead of "We're aware of this issue," **say**, *"We're working on this right now and hope to have it fixed very soon."*

Instead of "We appreciate your patience," **say,** *"Thanks so much for bearing with us while we fix this!"*

WHEN THINGS HAVE SETTLED DOWN:

Once the problem is identified and a fix is in the works or in place, make sure that every customer who reached out on social media gets a personal follow up response. All emails should get a detailed reply outlining the issue and offering to help more if needed. In addition to a sincere apology, **you absolutely must communicate to customers:**

- **Who** is affected
- **What** happened
- **When** it will be (or was) fixed
- **How** the app will change, improve, or recover so it doesn't happen again

AFTER THE FACT:

Communicate, communicate, *communicate*! Yes, downtime and bugs really suck, and no one wants to announce their failures to the world. But we are seeing more and more the companies that do choose to be transparent under attack are the companies that win customer loyalty through their sincerity, honesty, and openness. If you're going to invest money in an app or convince your entire company to use it, wouldn't you want to know that if it ever breaks you'd get an apology, an update, and a fix?

The best example I've ever seen of a company winning the war against a terrible situation is the response by social media app Buffer when it was hacked in 2013. Not only were they incredibly responsive on social media as things were happening, they were proactive in posting details of the hack on their company blog and in individual emails to customers. Yes—*they gave details of the failure* out to customers, the very thing most corporate big wigs would never, ever do!

Buffer didn't shy away from admitting the problem, and neither should you if you're ever in that situation. They didn't cloud the issue in big words or technical phrases, and they didn't leave customers questioning what was next or if their data was safe. *When you're in this position, be responsive, apologetic, and sincere.*

For some inspiration, here's **the entire** letter their founder Joel Gascoigne sent to each Buffer user after the hacking incident:

Hi there, I wanted to get in touch to apologize for the awful experience we've caused many of you on your weekend. Buffer was hacked around 1 hour ago, and many of you may have experienced spam posts sent from you via Buffer. I can only understand how angry and disappointed you must be right now. Not everyone who has signed up for Buffer has been affected, but you may want to check on your accounts. We're working hard to fix this problem right now and we're expecting to have everything back to normal shortly. We're posting continual updates on the Buffer Facebook page and the Buffer Twitter page to keep you in the loop on everything. The best steps for you to take right now and important information for you:

- *Remove any postings from your Facebook page or Twitter page that look like spam*
- *Keep an eye on Buffer's Twitter page and Facebook page*
- *Your Buffer passwords are not affected*
- *No billing or payment information was affected or exposed*
- *All Facebook posts sent via Buffer have been temporarily hidden and will reappear once we've resolved this situation*

I am incredibly sorry this has happened and affected you and your company. We're working around the clock right now to get this resolved and we'll continue to post updates on Facebook and Twitter. If you have any questions at all, please respond to this email. Understandably, a lot of people have emailed us, so we might take a short while to get back to everyone, but we will respond to every single email.

— Joel and the Buffer team

FEATURE REQUESTS

Question: *"Do we really have to reply to feature request emails or allow customers to post them on an open forum?"*

Answer: Yes. Yes and Yes.

There used to be a genius idea floating around the tech scene regarding product development for the web: *"Say no to feature requests."* The gist of the statement meant, *"Be confident in your design and don't load it up with a bunch of unnecessary features."*

The *tone*, however, revealed a much more antagonistic view of customers' ideas and opinions, and implied they just don't matter. The aggression behind the statement caused way too many people to interpret it as a mantra that supported ignoring customer emails, not having public customer forums, and slamming the door in the face of customers' ideas.

Well, we also used to charge for return shipping and send password reminders in plain text. Do those ideas still sound genius today?

Plain and simple: You need to reply to every customer email, call, chat or tweet, even if the customer is submitting a feature request you're not going to add. Having a public customer forum where people can cast votes for features is also a great way to stay on top of these requests without increasing email or chat volume. Ideally, your contact page should allow users to choose why they're contacting you, and filter them to the forum if they do have a request only.

Having a customer forum is a big way to encourage VIP feeling among your customers. Loyal users often have the most passionate ideas for your app, which can be intimidating and maybe even a bit annoying. But remember: They are a set of new eyes on a design that you are often too close to. Ask them what they want, ask them what they think, and rely on their ideas to help you develop your app.

Here are some scenarios and sample replies you can use to train your team on handling feature requests:

This request is a really good idea, and one we could possibly add later on.

First, make sure you reply to let the customer know you're listening. Thank them for taking the time to share their idea, and if you have a customer forum where you accept votes for features, send them over to add their idea. (Make sure you also have someone on staff moderating the forum, replying to each popular request, and marking each idea In Consideration or In Progress if it's something you're really thinking of adding.)

Sample replies:

- *"Great idea! Thanks for taking the time to send this one in."*
- *"Thanks for sharing your thoughts on this! Make sure you add this to our Customer Forum so other users can add their support for it."*
- *"Thanks for sharing this idea! It's one we've heard before, so we'll make sure it's on our list of features to consider when we're ready to make some changes."*

This idea is confusing or complicated, and you're not sure you'll add it.

Again, reply to let the customer know you're listening. Figure out *why* the customer wants this feature, how they'd use it in your app, or ask for some clarification so you can reply appropriately.

Sample replies:

- *"Thanks for sharing this idea! It helps to know how people are using our product and what they'd like to see added in the future. I'd love to hear more about why this would be useful to you."*
- *"This could definitely be an interesting feature to look into. Could you elaborate more on why you're looking for this feature or how exactly you'd use it?"*
- *"Thanks for sending in this idea! We can't always add new features that are requested, but we do keep track of each one. This may be something we look into later on down the line."*

This request is absurd or ridiculous or totally not going to happen. You literally don't know what this customer is thinking.

What's the pattern here? Oh yeah: *Reply to let the customer know you're listening.* Even if you know you can't add this feature idea, you still need to acknowledge it. The best solution for feature requests you know you will not add is to be upfront about it — make sure the customer knows *why* you can't add their idea and, if you really want to excel, suggest alternative products that offer what they're looking for.

Sample replies:

- *"Thanks for taking the time to outline this idea. I'm not sure it's something we'll be able to add, since it's not really in line with our plans for the product. But it is something we can circle back to if those plans change later on."*
- *"We don't have plans to offer this option right now, but it's definitely an idea we can come back to when we're adding features to a later version."*
- *"Since we may not be able to add this feature you need, you may want to check out ____, which does offer this feature standard."*

"The key is to set realistic customer expectations, and then not to just meet them, but to exceed them — preferably in unexpected and helpful ways."

— Richard Branson

BUILDING A HELP SECTION

Question: *"Do we need to launch our app with a big help section, or should we build it as we go along? Who should be in charge of keeping it updated?"*

Answer: Start with as much educational material as possible, and keep it fresh!

Listen here, tech founders: **Self-service is the future of customer support.**

Having easy-to-access educational materials online is *the only thing* that will reduce your support volume over time. Customers are loyal to products that are easy to use and easy to learn about, meaning there's a help section, tutorials, and videos easily accessible to them. Investing the time in creating a thorough, searchable help section is thinking ahead for your customers and your brand.

Let's say you have 100 customers and 5 of those customers have the same questions about your product. When you have 200 customers, 10 more people may have the same question. But let's say over the course of 6 months you suddenly find yourself with 10,000 active users. That will most likely mean 500 people who have the same question, which equates to 500 additional support requests for you to answer. If you're like me, you'd rather answer this question *one time,* not one thousand times.

Start with **10 simple questions** in a help section, and answer each with a detailed response and screenshots. From those 10 questions, create 10 more that are related. An average knowledge base for an app 6 months old or younger contains 30 FAQs and is searchable and categorized for easy perusal. For an app over 1 year old with more than 5,000+ active users, you'll need to have double that size help section and add on at least 3 in-depth tutorials or video walkthroughs.

If you don't have a lot of customer questions already, ask a friend, relative or colleague who's never used your app before to play around with it front of you. Watch which buttons they click first, write down every question they ask you, and try and see the product from a real new user's perspective, not just how you think a new user will act. You built your app so you have an idea of what you think people will ask you, but nothing will ever tell you *for sure* what questions people have except real user data.

If you have active customers contacting you for support, look for patterns in their questions and start tracing common support problems back to the root. If you answer the same question more than 3 times per week, it needs to be in your help section. *This isn't op-*

tional! The next time you're asked the same question, write your answer, then copy and paste it into your knowledge base *before* you send the reply email. From then on, instead of answering the question outright in your email, say to your customer, *"We've answered this in detail over in our help section!"* and send them the direct link.

While you're watching those patterns, track specific pain points by daily and monthly volume. How many times do people ask to recover their password? How many times to people complain that they can't find a tab or button inside your app? It may be annoying, but you may find that your own customers' questions can pinpoint a bad design decision in your product. By tracking what people ask you and keeping metrics—however rudimentary—you'll have a better understanding of how people use your product and how you can improve the product for their use.

Some people think that every support email reflects a failure in our product design. While that may not always be true, every support email does reflect what information is missing in our online education. If we start paying attention to what people are asking and have an open mind about it, we start to see where we can be better about explaining our intentions with our app, and make the learning curve shorter for new customers.

Maybe you're thinking this all sounds like too much work when you're already busy building the next Instagram for dog selfies. Well take heart—almost every help desk product offers a searchable knowledge base built right in; all you have to do is add the content. And think of it this way: Having a quick search box where a customer can search for their question and get your answer means they never have to write you a support email in the first place!

GETTING CUSTOMERS TO RTFM

Question: *"We have a ton of answers in our help section, but people still write us asking questions. How do we get them to read the freaking manual?"*

Answer: Write a better manual, and then tell people about it!

This can be one of the most frustrating parts of doing customer support—you spend all this time writing a great help section, and no one reads it. Come on! *How hard is it to click the Help link on a website?!*

As much as we want the future to be here now, there's still a large set of users who aren't used to self service or self education. Part of our job is letting them know that help exists beyond email and live chat, and making sure that when customers are navigating our help info they find what they're looking for. Here are a few ways to get more eyes on your awesome help material:

MAKE YOUR HELP SECTION FUN AND ENGAGING

It's still a common feeling that online help sections are boring, full of technical jargon and uninspiring blocks of text. People will actually *want* to read your user guide if it's interesting, so start by making it so! Don't be afraid to use casual, friendly language, insert appropriate jokes or funny images, or even hide easter eggs for customers to discover.

Want to really go for it? Think about adding translators to articles to convert them to pirate speak or LOL-Cat. Use gifs or small embedded videos in each article. Hide Fun Fact and trivia articles that have nothing to do with your product in your FAQ and give out discount codes to customers who find them.

HELP CUSTOMERS HELP THEMSELVES

Every time I reply to a support email with an answer that I know has been documented, I include a link to the article in my reply. This is a no-brainer! Remember that farming customers off to the help section isn't going to work if your help section isn't easy to use or if a customer feels like you're not answering the right question. Make sure you give their email the attention it needs, that you acknowledge their question, and let them know more details can be found at the help link.

Example: If a person asks me how to update their billing information, my response should be along the lines of *"You can update your billing information easily on the account tab. Here's an article on that from our help section: <link>"*

This answers the customer's question directly, gives them more information to go on, and hopefully leads them to find more answers to questions on their own.

ADVERTISE YOUR HELP LIKE IT'S IMPORTANT

Companies send newsletters out all the time linking to their Twitter feed or company blog. How many times have you added new help articles to your marketing material? If you're getting information in front of customers (newsletters, social media, blogs), consider your help section as another way to advertise your company. If it's informative and interesting, people will be drawn to it.

Try adding links to new help articles or tutorials in your email signature, or even mentioning them on Twitter. It will remind customers that you're proactive in offering self-education and direction. If you're enthusiastic about what you're putting out there, customers will be much more interested in checking it out.

USE AN INTUITIVE HELP DESK TO HOST YOUR ONLINE RESOURCES OR KNOWLEDGE BASE AND CONTACT FORM.

Most modern help desks allow you to host your knowledge base and contact forms in the same channel. This can be extremely helpful in cutting down support emails since the contact form and help section are linked. When a customer chooses to email you using the embedded contact form, the help desk will match keywords present in them with related help articles before sending the email. Keep in mind, this won't work unless you first keep your help section up to date and use tags to match alternate keywords.

Your help articles should be clear and concise, and anticipate questions customers are going to have. If I'm having trouble with my login, I may search for "log in," "login," "username," "password," or "account." By using keywords and tags on articles, you can help customers get the information they need more quickly. If you're going to host your own knowledge base or help section, make sure it has some search capability.

SOCIAL SUPPORT

Question: *"Should we offer customer support on social media? Do we need to hire a community manager or should our support team handle it?"*

Answer: Always, and if not always, most times.

A few years ago, customer support was partitioned from social media, which was typically handled by marketing *gurus*. Today, customer support is a part of everything your company does, from product development and marketing to its social presence. There's no longer a huge dissimilarity between customer support and community managers — both are directly engaging with customers on a daily basis and should be empowered to handle praise and crisis publicly.

The typical breakdown is that customer support agents handle mostly email or chat support, while community managers are in charge of social or public streams (Twitter, Facebook, Instagram, or customer forums). You don't need to have fiercely delineated roles if you're a smaller company or if you want to keep all your customer support activity in one place. If you have a larger support team consider a rotating schedule for employees so everyone has a chance to jump in on social streams weekly.

Your customer support team should be active on social media daily, not weekly and not a few times per month. Brands that consistently excel at social support have a few things in common: They are quickly responsive, pro-active, consistent, and *fun*. If you focus on those main qualities, you'll find that investing in social support is a huge win for your customers and your brand.

DOING SOCIAL RIGHT

- **Be quick!** The number one rule for social support is *responsiveness*. Think of public customer posts high priority and respond as fast as you can. For an active Twitter or Facebook account, you should aim for a response time of less than an hour, and you should respond to every post. If you set a precedent of being responsive when there isn't a crisis, customers will know they can reach out when there is one and get help quickly.
- **Don't deflect unless you have to.** Customers will reach out to you on Twitter because that's where *they* want to resolve their problem. Most of the time customers have already tried to reach out via email or phone, and are going to social media because they believe it will lead to a faster resolution. In 2013, Conversocial reported[3] that 76% of social conversations between customers and brands ended completely after they asked the customer switch

3 *"Tweet, Email or Call: Which Brands are Re-directing Social Media Complaints to Traditional Channels."*

channels. Asking customers to follow up via phone or email should be a last resort, only if you're unable to fix their issue without doing so.

- **Don't just copy and paste.** You will have the urge to do this when you're fighting through downtime or a massive bug, but the last thing customers want to see when they go to your social stream is the same few sentences, pasted over and over to every customer. If you do need to distribute the same info to a bunch of customers, consider making a few public posts, then replying to customers with a personal message and a link to those posts. Make sure you use the customer's name whenever you can, and give them as much info as possible.
- **Use social media daily, not only in crisis or for promotion**. The worst thing that can happen to your Twitter stream is letting it become an apology vacuum, or devolve into a bulletin board for expired coupons and closed contests. You should try to engage with your customers daily by replying to every post. Set up lists and alerts to track conversations relating to your brand, your product, or people searching for something your app can do.
- **Be friendly and fun**. One of my all-time favorite Twitter accounts isn't what you'd expect, it's fast food chain Taco Bell. I am a huge fan of their social media tactics and I've never even eaten at a Taco Bell in my life! What sets Taco Bell's tweets apart is their informal, conversational tone with anyone

who mentions them, even if it's a customer complaining. Other top Twitter accounts you can learn from are JetBlue, XBox Support, Chase Support, Verizon, and Home Depot.

- **Find your voice.** While being fun and jokey won't work for every brand in every circumstance, setting a tone with your social posts will help give your brand a personality that customers can identify with. Look to well-known brands that share your philosophies to determine better ways you can be engaging with your customers. **Remember:** You want to set the tone for *your* company, not just mimic another brand. Take the best of what other companies do and evolve it to fit yours.

PRIORITIZING SUPPORT

Question: *"What's the best way to prioritize our support queue, or manage a shared inbox and social streams?"*

Answer: The only word you need to learn is *triage.*

Starting the day with a messy inbox is every support person's nightmare. Learning how to prioritize daily volume requests will not only make you feel more organized and in control, it will also make you a better product manager. It's easy to want to start at the bottom and handle oldest issues first, but those aren't always the most important emails for you to tackle each day.

Here's a primer on triaging your inbox and setting priorities on the types of emails you're getting each day:

FIRST: BUG REPORTS, BILLING DISPUTES, AND TECH ISSUES.

When you peruse your inbox each morning, look for any pattern of complaints. Are multiple people experience the same bug? Is someone saying they lost their work or that a feature is missing? Take time to read through all of these and try to replicate the issue on your own, then give the customer an immediate reply. You shouldn't wait to reply until after you've fixed an issue—that could take hours. If you don't have an immediate fix, tell the customer you're working on it and will get back to them with a resolution. If your app runs on multiple platforms that are web-based, make sure your help documentation includes tips for all the various browsers, including how to clear cache and cookies, updating plugins, and where to download updates.

Billing disputes or complaints should be handled as a first priority as well, since anything related to money is a hot button issue.

SECOND: ANY HOW-TO OR "DOES YOUR PRODUCT DO X" REQUEST.

Move on to less pressing issues that fall into an educational category. Any time a person asks you, *"How do I ..."* you have an opportunity to make your documentation better. As a general rule, anything customers ask you more than twice a week needs to go in your Help section. The next time you get one of these requests, write your answer and create a knowledge base article about it before sending the email. If don't have the time to write a full help section right away, adding questions your customers ask you will develop your knowledge base over time.

THIRD: FEATURE REQUESTS OR WISH LIST ITEMS FOR YOUR PRODUCT.

Don't be defensive about feature requests or any other wish list items your customers send to you. You may have very specific ideas about features your product needs, and a philosophy of how your customers should use it, but that may not always translate when your app is in the wild. Instead of being annoyed or shooting down the customer's idea, think of it as a way to see your product the way your customers do. Don't worry—thanking your customers for their idea doesn't promise you'll implement it. It shows your customers that you're listening, that you have *their* best interest in mind, and you are willing to adjust the product if you need to down the line. If you're using a customer forum, make sure to have customers post their suggestions so you can keep track of new ideas and so other customers can vote on them.

When you know what customers are asking of you and requesting of your app, you'll automatically prioritize new features and bug fixes that matter to your audience. You won't learn anything from your customers without keeping track of what they are asking you.

GENERAL PRAISE AND POSITIVE RESPONSES.

Of course you'll be happy to answer these emails, but why stop there when a customer has taken the time to contact you with glowing praise? Dedicate some time each week to acknowledging these responses in your social media posts (it's as easy as searching for your customer on Twitter and sending a public reply). And don't be shy about asking vocal customers to take their praise to the app store—those 4 stars can't hurt!

TRIAGING WHILE SHARING AN INBOX

If you're working on a team that shares an inbox, assign one person to be your team lead and have that person triage all day. This person should triage all emails coming in and distribute them appropriately to your team, making sure that all team members are handling an equal set of tickets. (Remember that it's not just about numbers but difficulty level; one team member may handle 100 easy questions to another member's 50 difficult questions.) Rotate the position so each team member is lead for at least one week a month.

SCALING SUPPORT

Question: *"How will we know when and how to ramp up our support offerings? Should we hire a big team right away?"*

Answer: Focus on educating your customers well, and hire before you need to.

The lifecycle of app development is pretty standard: You come up with an idea, hire a designer, hire some programmers, then take it to market. Rarely is customer support part of this equation from the very beginning. Support is actually *almost always* an afterthought, and it becomes a priority only when you're suddenly drowning in support tickets, complaints, or feature requests. So what's the best way to prepare for this onslaught once your app hits the market and people start using it?

Scaling support starts with determining what level of support your app is going to offer from the very beginning. You'll need to buckle down and decide on actual support methods: Should we offer phone support? Email only? What about using Twitter for support, and if we do use Twitter, should it be a separate support account? Does Facebook matter?

If you're struggling to figure out where customer support fits in your app development stage, here's a quick primer to know when and why you should scale your support:

PHASE I

You have a brand new app or product in private beta or limited launch, or you've launched to a small audience. Even though you may not have a lot of customers yet, you still need to reply to every email and every mention in social media. Get to know your customers by name.

Use their questions to build your online knowledge base and feature links to your help section prominently in new signup emails, billing emails, and in your own email signature. (This can be the most important part of your initial support offering since 40% of most customer questions can be answered by a help article!) Let customers know you take their input seriously and would love to know their thoughts on using the app, and take swift action to apologize if things go down or bugs surface. If you're seeing fewer than 20 support emails per day, using a free email service like Gmail is ideal.

PHASE II

You'll need to move into this phase when you're getting around 60 emails per day, but no more than 80 on a regular basis. You've taken your app to market and have a steady flow of new customers each day. You're starting to get more support emails and more followers on Twitter, and maybe even a Facebook fan page. This is the time to start hiring up your support team to make sure you have enough hands on deck.

Your product development team should interact daily with your support team to learn how customers are using your product, what they're asking for, and what experience can be improved. You should be able to answer all customer emails in 24 hours as a standard, but aim for a response time of 2-3 hours. Integrating live chat, outbound call support (where *you* call the customer), and a support-centric Twitter feed is also a necessity at this stage. Use the immediacy of Twitter to your advantage to meet customers where they are and keep email volume low. Consider ramping up to use a full-scale help desk tool that offers a built-in knowledge base and customer feedback forum for users to submit ideas.

PHASE III

At this stage, you've had paying customers for a while, and you're getting over 100 emails per day. A good rule is hiring one support agent for every 60 unique cases you get per day. Your support agents should maintain the turn-around time you've set as an SLA with customers, and you should have published business hours for your support team so your customers know when they're available to help. Your customer forum should be up and running and engaging customers publicly, and your support Twitter feed should show more replies to customers than anything else.

Your customer support team should be expected to curate your knowledge base daily, and to keep track of common feature requests to take back to your development team. Encourage your CEO or founder to pop into help with support once a week or more to stay engaged with new customers and personally interact with long-time loyal customers again. Consider sending personal emails to your first few customers who are still with you, or calling the most vocal customers in your forums to chat about your product roadmap.

At the end of the day, what matters is that you think of customer support as an essential part of your whole app development. If you're working by yourself and outsourcing development or design, consider implementing one or two support options every 6 months until you're ready to bring on more full-time help. If you offer support prominently your customers will know that they're important to you and reward you with their loyalty.

"Traditional corporations, particularly large-scale service and manufacturing businesses, are organized for efficiency. Or consistency. But not joy. Joy comes from surprise and connection and humanity and transparency and new… If you fear special requests, if you staff with cogs, if you have to put it all in a manual, then the chances of amazing someone are really quite low."

– Seth Godin

SUPPORT BY FOUNDERS

Question: *"I'm a founder doing support. What's the best way for me to stay on top of everything? When will I know it's time to hire a dedicated support team?"*

Answer: Plan ahead, manage your time, and turn it over when it's no longer fun.

DOING IT YOURSELF.

If you're development-centric, you know your focus needs to be on just that: development. If you have to integrate into your daily schedule writing user guides, replying to customer emails, monitoring social media, and reading app store reviews, you're never going to get anything else done. You have to create a balance where you can be involved with support without it taking over your schedule.

Here are a few proactive tips if you're running a product and focusing on customer support at the same time:

- **Start with a really clear, friendly online help section.** If you answer obvious questions in advance, you cut out the potential for anyone to email you for an obvious answer. When you reply to emails, point people back to the answer in your online Help section so they can educate themselves on their own. Make sure your knowledge base is searchable so customers can easily find answers.

- **Create friendly email scripts to cut your replying time in half.** You can save yourself 40 hours a month of typing if you have templates for your most commonly used responses. But the key here is to use templates that are real and human, not auto replies or anything that sounds like a robot is writing. Templates should include things like, *"Hi ___, Thanks for trying our app!"* and *"Sorry to hear you're running into this trouble."* Fill in the blanks with an answer for a customer, and use a signature block to add something like, *"Let me know if you need anything else!"* (**Pro tip:** Include your name in a signature block so you don't spend all day typing your own name over and over.)
- **Engage your community from day one.** Creating an online forum for customers is an awesome way to encourage early adopters' enthusiasm for your product. It also keeps a record of early problems, questions and issues that can turn into help section articles, and gives you access to a built in "beta" release team for future versions.
- **Assess common support requests monthly and squash them.** Spend 2-4 hours a month looking back on common support requests and identifying areas for improvement in your app. It could be a

design decision that isn't going over well or a missing feature you need to seriously consider adding. "Fixing" issues at the root cause early on prevents a back log of issues later when your customer base is much bigger and more vocal.

WHEN TO TURN IT OVER.

There is always going to be a huge gap between being overwhelmed with doing all the customer support yourself and having the resources to hire a support person full-time. Hiring a support person is a big investment, and sometimes it's just not in the budget. If you're thinking you may need help with support but aren't quite sure, answer a few questions to see where you stand:

- Does answering support emails take more than 2 hours of your time each day?
- Do you find yourself putting off support until the end of the day or cringe when you think of what's waiting for you?
- Have you found yourself getting defensive in your replies or agitated with customers who ask too many questions?
- Are simple questions about your app annoying to answer day after day?

If you answered "Yes" to any of these, stop what you're doing and hire a dedicated support person to take over for you. It's time to hand it over when it becomes an actual burden for you and you find that you're just not enjoying it anymore. The worst thing you could do is allow the customer experience to suffer because you're afraid to let go.

When you consider hiring in for support, keep these tips in mind to make sure your customer experience is just as great as when you do it yourself:

- **Find someone like you.** Hiring is hard, but we've learned over the years that it's better to hire for personality than just for skill. Hiring someone who is like you will help you feel more comfortable handing over the reigns. Ask the potential support person how they'd handle a certain situation, or even give them example questions you're asked daily to answer during their application process. Great minds think alike, and you'll probably learn more about a person this way than by asking them boring and bland interview questions.
- **Train, train, train.** Then train some more. Whoever you hire to do support is only as good as what they know, so it's your job to make sure they have the resources to know everything about your product and process. Make sure they are kept up to date with all new versions & updates, and that they have a searchable help section to refer to for questions about the app. And make sure you're available to help train them more and answer questions, and that means ...

- **Stay in constant communication with your support person.** You decided to hire someone to do support so you wouldn't have to be involved, right? Wrong! Your product depends on your leadership and so will your customer support. By staying in touch with whomever is handling your support, you make the process less like someone hired to watch an email box and more like a member of your product team. If you're working remotely, consider using HipChat, Slack or Hall as an internal chatroom your whole team is a part of each day. Encourage your support person to ask questions and reach out to developers for help with technical issues, so everyone sees what questions are being asked.
- **Set clear expectations for how you want customer support to be run.** There's nothing worse than being totally disappointed with an employee, but remember: Disappointment is just expectation not verbalized. Avoid any disappointment or miscommunication by setting clear goals for your support person and leave nothing to chance. Set exact times you expect support emails to be replied to by, outline specific words you don't want a person to use, and make sure they have a crisis plan in place in case things go down and you're not immediately available.

REFUNDS

Question: *"Should we give refunds to customers just because they ask for it?"*

Answer: Always, and if not always, most times.

Refunds are always a sticky situation because once money has been exchanged for goods, no one really wants to give that money back. But if we take a look at some of the most successful service-oriented companies, we'll find that all of them have lenient return and refund policies. Most will now pay for return shipping on physical items and process refunds once the shipping label is tracked, before they even receive the item from you! Now *that's* awesome service.

Customers are beginning to expect this leniency with all companies and products, and it's difficult to say a blanket "*no*" to a refund request. These days, having an absolute no refunds policy is antiquated and downright hostile to customers, and could be a deciding factor when customers are choosing whether to recommend your service.

Let's be realistic: we can't just give away money. But you can find a way to please angry customers, appease frustrated customers, and win their favor with your generosity.

- **Make your policy prominent.** If you don't have a clear and concise refund policy stated on your website, it's going to be difficult to enforce. Bundling your refund policy in your terms of service isn't going to cut it—you need to explicitly state refund terms prominently in your help section. If you can, add it to product and checkout pages.
- **Set boundaries for leniency.** If you're going to offer refunds on a case-by-case basis, make sure you have more than a gut feeling to go on. Consider the length of time a customer has used the product, whether their account has been inactive, and what their reasoning behind their refund request is.
- **If a customer doesn't like it, let them go.** Customers don't want to be haggled, especially if they aren't satisfied with a product. If a customer decides your product just isn't for them, let them go gracefully. A quick and no-questions refund offer impresses customers and may even win them back later on.
- **Offer credits in lieu of cash**. If your product is subscription or use-based, consider offering a month free in lieu of a straightforward refund.
- **Use license keys for digital goods to restrict use after refunds.** If a customer has purchased digital goods, it's nearly impossible to refund a purchase and verify they can't use the product again. If you're able to, use license keys to limit access to digital goods once a refund has transpired, and make sure the customer knows they won't have access to their purchase if they choose a refund.

DISCOUNTS, COUPONS, & PEOPLE WHO WON'T PAY

Question: *"How should we reply if people ask for student or non-profit discounts, or a coupon code? Are we required to offer non-profit pricing?"*

Answer: People will always ask for discounts, and you can acquiesce or decline gracefully. It's your choice to offer discounts, but lean towards being generous and thoughtful whenever you can and be honest when you cannot.

It's inevitable that you'll be asked for a special student rate on your product, or a free version for a non-profit organization. Many companies do choose to discount products but for those who don't, saying no can be awkward and tricky.

If you want to offer discounts to nonprofits or students, make sure your discount is manually applied, or that you offer a personalized and trackable code. (Otherwise, you risk that code being shared with anyone!) You may want to consider giving the code and expiration date, or offering a specific timeframe in which to use it.

The best option for subscription-based web apps is to offer free time, or by crediting an account without refunding or discounting any fees. If your app offers a free trial, consider extending the trial 2-4 weeks. You can also offer to add features normally only offered in upgraded accounts to a customer's lower paying account.

Alternatives to discounts:

- **Discount time.** Offer to extend a free trial after signup, or offer a month free if the customer is an established user.
- **Tell your friends.** Give a referral-based discount code the customer can distribute themselves.
- **This for that.** If you do choose to offer a discounted or free account, ask the customer to write up a blog post or interview them about how they're using your product.
- **Free features.** Offer to add access to premium features to a lower paid account.

Sample replies:

- *"Unfortunately, we're not offering discounts at this time, but we often publicize coupon codes for existing customers on our social media accounts."*
- *"We've priced our products fairly so they're economical for all types of businesses, including nonprofits."*
- *"We believe all our prices are fair and reasonable, and we also offer a free version that you'll never be charged to use. To treat all our customers equally, we aren't offering discounts at this time."*

IRATE & ABUSIVE CUSTOMERS

Question: *"What should we do if customers become irate or downright abusive? Are we obligated to reply to them?"*

Answer: Plan in advance what your support team will accept from customers, and make sure they're empowered to diffuse or shut down any inappropriate communication.

There will be days when it seems like every customer you interact with is out to get you. While that's most likely not the case, it will sure feel like it, and that can impact your interactions with other customers in a bad way. If you're having one of those bad days, here are some tips for keeping your cool and turning things around.

DEALING WITH IRATE CUSTOMERS

- **Allow the customer to vent if they need to.** Sometimes people just need to state their frustrations to anyone who'll listen. Their issues may not even be about you, but you may be the easy target for their venting. Make sure that you let them get it all out, then let them know you're there to help, and you're both on the same side.

- **Use gentle language in reply.** A great way to turn around a tense conversation is to reply in a differing tone. If a customer is being irate and you reply defensively or curtly, the situation will only devolve from there. For your first reply, try to use gentle, empathetic language and use a "Kill them with kindness" approach. It can be easy as saying, *"I'm sorry you're having a rough day. Let me see how I can help."*
- **Don't take it personally.** Keep in mind that it's not about you, really. It may feel like it, but to the customer, you're just the person who happens to be there listening to them rant. Don't internalize the situation and let it compromise your attitude or how you respond to other customers.
- **Take a walk before you reply.** It's the oldest trick in the book, and it works for a reason. When you're in a heated discussion, distancing yourself from it will renew your patience and perspective. If you can't *literally* take a walk, work with other customers to put some space between you and the conflict.
- **Ask a colleague to review the interaction and assess the next move.** If you feel like you aren't getting anywhere with an irate customer, have someone else take a look at the correspondence. They may be able to pinpoint where it went wrong and give you insight for a resolution. You may even want to consider developing a hierarchy on your team where

you pass off emails to another teammate when you aren't able to resolve it on your own.

- **If a customer becomes abusive, give them a warning then shut them down.** No support agent should have to endure any abuse from customers, and that includes name-calling, inappropriate advances, threats, and the use of agitated profanity. If your first replies don't turn the situation around and a customer continues to rage on you, give them a warning. Tell them you'll be happy to help them more, but you won't be able to do that if they continue to be abusive or inappropriate.
- **Pass them on.** Have a system in place to escalate the worst offenders to a manager. Know your limits and act on them—if you feel a customer's out of line and you can't appease them, don't feel bad about escalating the issue, ceasing communication, or even terminating that customer's account. If possible, make sure your terms of service indicate that abusive and threatening language will not be tolerated by your support team.

If your attitude is compromised

- **Breathe deep.** If you feel like a bad customer interaction is spoiling your day, pause for a moment and reflect. The worst thing that can happen is allowing one bad interaction—even if it's really, really bad—to color how you respond to other customers.

- **Express gratitude.** If you're in a funk, make a list of things you're grateful for off the top of your head. Don't think too much about it, just let the gratitude flow. You'll find thinking of things you're thankful for will help turn your mood around. (Burning incense and playing Hacky Sack may also help, but we don't want to turn you into a hippie just yet.)
- **Help someone else.** Turn your attention to another customer you can help or a teammate who can use your input. Finding solutions and solving problems can vastly improve your day!
- **Tackle other tasks.** If you're just not in the best mood to be interacting with customers, work on another constructive task for a while. Update your help section, write a blog post, or run through some ideas that can help improve your support process.

INCREASING PRICES & PIVOTING

Question: *"How do we communicate to customers that we have to increase our prices, or that we're changing the direction of our product?"*

Answer: Be honest, upfront, timely and sincere.

Sharing uncomfortable news with customers is never easy, and two of the hardest things to communicate are an increase in pricing or a major change to a product. The best way to tackle these issues are by being upfront with customers the moment you know something will change, and explain as clearly as possible why the change was made. Don't be afraid to inform customers tfor the reasons of your price increase. There is no reason to wait on sharing this info — the moment you know a change is on the horizon, let your customers know.

If you're shifting the direction of your company, write out a detailed explanation you can share with customers if they write in to complain, and publish it publicly on your company site or blog. State the answers to any questions you'd have if a company you were a customer of suddenly changed direction— what's next for current customers? Will they be refunded? How much will actually change?

A while back I got an email from Saddleback Leather's CEO Dave, with the subject line "An Important Letter" and this intro:

> *"Dave here. I have something important to tell you. It's not the most enjoyable message to give you. So here it is. We're doing a price increase and there are some real good reasons why."*

The rest of the almost 1,400 word letter went on to explain the price increase, why it's necessary, how vendors are affected and supply has gotten scarce and how it's difficult to pass on that cost to the company but there's a good reason for it and all customers should know the details. This wasn't just a mass email that said *"Your new plan now costs $XX"*, it was a personal email from the guy in charge.

Saddleback took a really bad situation — a huge increase in prices— and turned it into a way to have a friendly and honest conversation with their customers. The email closed by stating some new improvements to handle stock requests, support and customer care for international customers, then ended with, *"I'm glad you're on the inside with us."* What a beautiful thing to tell a paying customer, past or present.

This is exactly how you should think about speaking to your customers in everything you write, not as "users" or computers or social media targets, but as new friends you want to have a long-lasting relationship with. The next time you have something uncomfortable to share with your customers, steal from Saddleback's approach. Your customers will love it, you'll probably feel better yourself about saying it, and we'll be that much closer to making the world a better place.

Admitting Mistakes—
Email over billing
ERROR

EMPTY VS. FULL WORDS

Want to immediately revamp the way you communicate with customers? Start with curating your daily language. Remove robotic and common *empty* words and add more sincere and human *full* words.

EMPTY WORDS - *Avoid using!*

- Feedback
- Inconvenience
- This issue
- That isn't, this isn't, we don't,
- No, We're unable to, I can't

FULL WORDS - *Use often!*

- Thank you!
- I'm really sorry
- This sucks, I know this is frustrating
- You're right, That's a great idea!
- Let me check and get back to you
- Thanks for sharing your idea, your thoughts, taking the time to help improve the app

IF THIS, THEN THAT

Instead of "I apologize," **say**, *"I'm really sorry."*

Instead of "I apologize for the inconvenience," **say**, *"I know this is frustrating and I'm very sorry."*

Instead of "Thank you for your feedback," **say**, *"Thanks so much for sharing your thoughts on this."*

Instead of "We appreciate your patience," **say**, *"Thanks so much for bearing with us!"*

Instead of "We're aware of this issue," **say**, *"We're working on this right now and hope to have it fixed very soon."*

Instead of "We don't have an ETA for a fix," **say**, *"We're working on it and I will get back to you soon with more info."*

SURPRISE & DELIGHT

- Send handwritten notes! (Invest in a good pen and a stress ball!) Send personal notes or emails on customer's anniversaries using your app, or thank you notes to your first 100 customers who are still active.
- Profile customers and how they use your product on your blog or social media pages.
- Offer % discounts for customers after they pass the year mark, and every anniversary after that.
- Follow top customers on social media and send them thank you gifts relevant to their interests (not company swag!)
- If you do send swag, make sure it's inclusive and fun. Who wants a corporate pen when you could send a beer koozie with your logo on it?
- Offer discounts for referrals, or set up an affiliate program that earns your customers account credit.
- Are your customers local? Show up in person with a gift pack to introduce yourself! (Don't be creepy.)
- Include funny gifs or pictures in support emails when you have a good rapport with a customer.
- Post contests on your blog and offer account credits to anyone who participates (not just the winner!).

- Refund the last billing or credit accounts when a customer has had a frustrating support experience, even if they don't ask. (If they do ask, maybe give more than they ask for!)

APOLOGIZE BETTER

- Be sincere, heartfelt, and honest, and take as much responsibility as possible.
- Don't say anything you wouldn't want to hear if you were the customer or hide behind technical jargon or legalese.

Instead of "I apologize," **say**, *"I'm really sorry."*

Instead of "We're sorry for the inconvenience," **say**, *"I understand your frustration and I'm very sorry this happened."*

Instead of "We appreciate your patience," **say**, *"Thanks so much for bearing with us while we fix this!"*

Power replies:

- *"You're right, we could definitely do this better."*
- *"Thanks for being open and honest about your experience so we can learn from it."*
- *"I really appreciate you helping us improve our process—we don't want this to happen again."*
- *"I know this is a huge disruption to your day and I'm working to get it fixed."*

BETTER WORDS TO USE

EMPATHETIC PHRASES:

- I completely understand
- I'm very sorry this is happening
- I see exactly what you mean
- You're right

ALTERNATE WORDS FOR INCONVENIENCE:

- Trouble
- Hassle
- Issue
- Frustration
- Irritation
- Disruption
- Annoyance

ALTERNATE WORDS FOR FEEDBACK:

- Thoughts
- Ideas

- Comments
- Review
- Input

WHAT MAKES A GREAT SUPPORT SYSTEM?

....

- Put the **customer's** experience first.

- Establish support systems that give employees clear instructions for gaining and maintaining service superiority. ✓ *We do this*

- Have passion for the customer's experience.

- Always strive to be the best.

- Give your support team a seat at the table. Get your entire team involved in development and give them a voice when it comes to adding new features, fixing bugs, and changing policies. ✓

- Put the customer's experience first.

- Allow your support team to make big decisions that benefit the customers. Empower them to be a voice for your company.

- Foster open communication on your team daily. ✓

- Encourage your support team to experiment, innovate, and share ideas with the whole company.

- Value your customers by being honest, upfront, and dependable.

- Celebrate team wins as much as possible.
- Grow a team of leaders by developing a company-wide vision for the customer experience.
- Put the customer's experience first!

MAKING YOUR TEAM CULTURE THRIVE

· ·

- Recognize when a team member has had a great customer interaction and highlight team member accomplishments for the whole company. *Jay*

- Reward small things: great responses to difficult customer questions, following up after bad experiences, taking initiative to clear the inbox or reply first on customer forums.

- Foster an environment of open communication, empathy, and honesty.

- Lead by example—your team members will be influenced by your attitude, your enthusiasm and your sincerity!

- Don't keep score—some people will answer emails faster than others, and some will take on writing more help articles. It's ok if the breakdown isn't uniform across the board as long as everyone pulls their weight and contributes time and energy equally. *different type of team work - we all do diff things*

- Don't hold grudges! Get grievances out in the open *+ have diff goals* and resolve them fast.

- Encourage team members to get to know each other genuinely and not by force. Culture is organic, not prescribed.
- Celebrate personal milestones, life changes, and non-work events.
- Remember that you're all in this together!

PHONE SUPPORT TIPS

When asked, "*What business practice would make you consider a different vendor?*" respondents stated the following:

- Scripted greetings (having your agents read out a highly structured greeting and engagement script): **31%** Agree - I've had to do this & hated this
- Hiding your phone number: **21%** — ?
- Asking for detailed contact information ("what is your name, account number, email") before helping them: **20%** 50% agree
- If you're going to publish your phone number, answer calls fast! Don't leave people hanging, and don't direct them automatically to a voicemail.
- Ask permission before requesting account details.
- Be friendly and casual, not robotic.
- Use the customer's name a lot! — Don't agree
- Explain to the customer why you're transferring them or why you're asking for specific information.
- Allow the customer to vent, and listen empathetically, even if it takes a while. — Yes
- Ask if you can call the customer back so they don't have to wait while you research. yes

- Follow up all calls with an email summarizing the solution for the customer. —yes

TIPS FOR HIRING

- **Recruit people who've had high empathy jobs.** Baristas, bartenders, librarians and bookshop employees are all excellent recruits for customer support roles. Their experience is usually in high-traffic positions where they are pulled in several directions at once and need to maintain empathy under pressure. This translates great to a support role that requires multitasking, problem solving, and thoughtful responses.
- **Include sample questions in your job ads.** Don't rely on cover letters and resumes to prove a person is a good writer, and don't wait until the interview to see if they can problem solve. Require that all applicants answer 3-4 sample questions based on real customer support inquiries about your app. It gives your applicants an opportunity to research your app and your published help resources and showcase what their approach to an actual customer would be like.
- **Look for people specifically motivated by helping *others.*** Do strangers randomly ask them for directions, for example? Do they speak highly of collaborative experiences rather than competitive ones?
- **When interviewing, uncover something that the person is passionate about.** How do they talk about

it? Do they get us excited about it? Can they articulate why they love it?

- **Hire before you need to.** Don't wait until you're underwater to hire more support help. Bring someone on before you're overwhelmed so there's time to train well and acclimate.

WRITE BETTER EMAILS!

BIG TIPS:

- Always use the customer's name in your greeting!
- Use contractions; don't try to be "professional." ← working on this
- Read your email out loud.
- Write each email like you would to a friend or parent.
- Encourage conversation.
- Clarify the problem by repeating it in different words.
- Be empathetic first, fast second.
- If you don't know the answer, say you don't know the answer but you'll find out.
- Reply to the customer while you're working on an issue.
- Overdose on *Thank You*'s — hm?
- Save the ;) , use better language instead. hm?
- Don't take it personally.

MAGIC PHRASES:

- *"You're right."*
- *"I'd love to help with this."*
- *"I can fix this for you."*
- *"Let me look into this for you."*
- *"I'll keep you updated."*
- *"Thanks for being our customer!"*

THE COSUPPORT MANIFESTO

Customers deserve better. They deserve your time and attention and empathy.

Feedback is the sound a microphone makes when it gets too close to a speaker. Is that noise what you call your customer's ideas?

Stop saying no and start saying maybe.

Tell an angry customer, *"You're right"* and watch what happens.

If you want to sell your product, start by selling your service. Is your support team available and accessible? Friendly? Fast? Thoughtful?

Speed matters. Don't wait to reply. If you don't know the answer right away, you can still reply to your customer and let them know you'll find out.

Keep the corporate-speak to yourself. Professional language isn't for customers. Be friendly, casual, accessible and fun.

Use better language. Mean what you say and say what you feel.

Feature requests aren't annoying, they prove someone likes what you built and they want to use it more. Stop being so defensive.

It's not possible to over-communicate. Give as much information as possible. Eliminate customer support needs by supporting customers first.

You're a human, not a robot. Customers are human, too. What a coincidence!

Thank your customers profusely.

Coupons for new users only are annoying and disrespectful. Celebrate loyalty and passionate users.

Surprising and delighting doesn't mean spending big bucks. Start with providing clear, concise instructions, a thorough help section, and self-education for all your users.

Stop apologizing for the inconvenience. Say you're sorry and mean it.

Listen more, then listen better.

Go big with service or go home.

ABOUT THE AUTHOR

CoSupport

Sarah Hatter is an author, public speaker, and entrepreneur. She's well known in the tech industry for her work focusing on the importance of customer experience and brand strategy. She produces conferences and events under the Elevate banner 4 times a year.

Sarah founded her consulting company CoSupport in 2011, and since then has become a sought after voice on the conference and teaching circuit for her unique perspective on building products with empathy for customers.

Her public speaking career has lead her to present privately at Microsoft, Google, Facebook, and leading tech conferences such as MicroConf and the Business of Software Conference.

Since 2012, CoSupport has produced **Elevate Summit events**, a bi-annual conference for customer support and customer experiennce professionals:

www.elevatesummit.co

They also have a podcast for support pros:

www.elevatesummit.co/podcast

Elevate Leaders, no-bullshit leadership conference for tech leaders:

www.elevateleaders.co

And **Elevate Women**, a community and leadership conference for women in tech and social entrepreneurs:

www.elevatewomen.org